AF581085

THE ROYALS
TUDORS TO WINDSORS

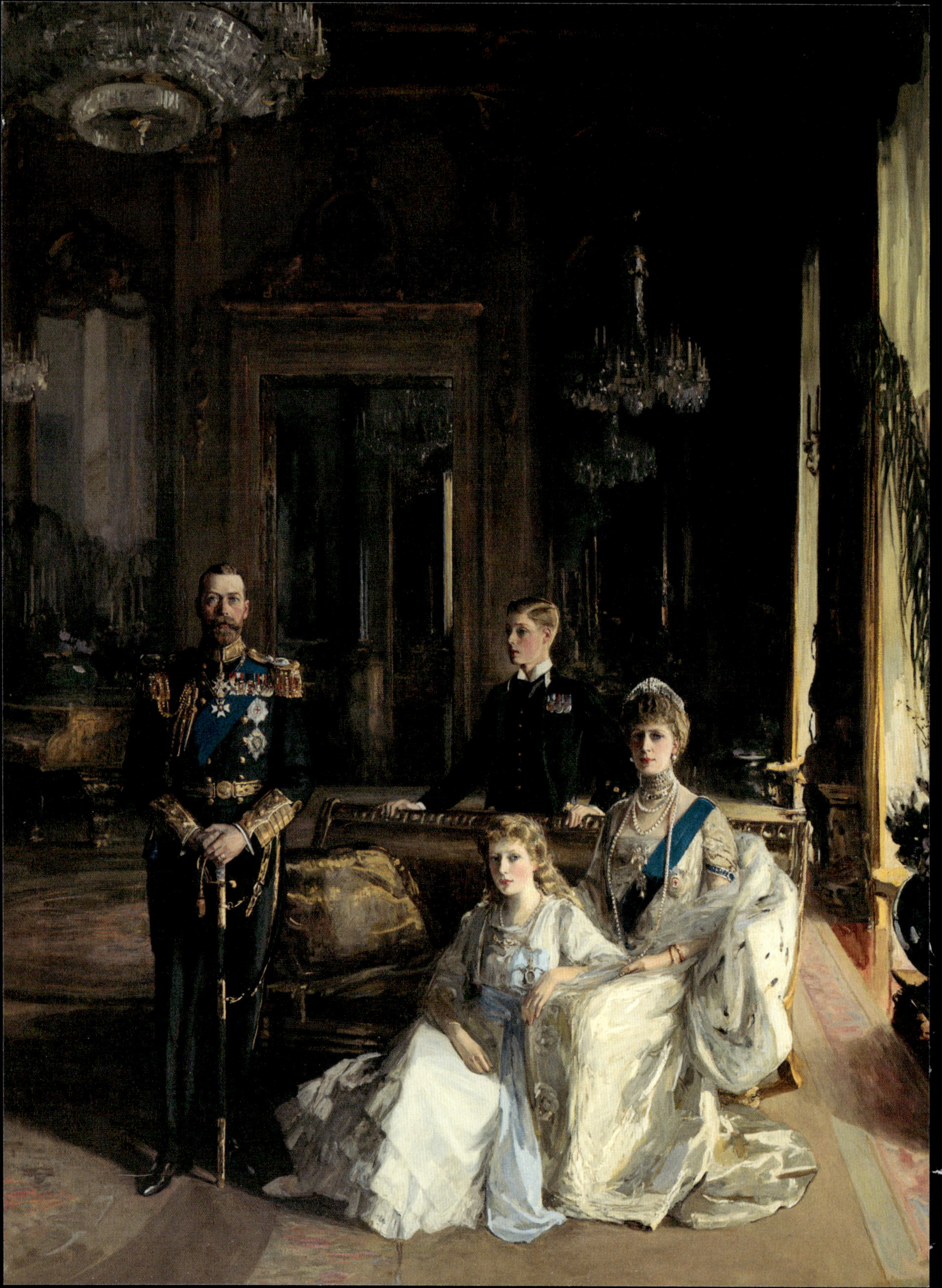

THE ROYALS
TUDORS TO WINDSORS

INTRODUCTION BY RAB MACGIBBON

NATIONAL PORTRAIT GALLERY, LONDON

Previous spread (detail)
'THE ROYAL FAMILY AT BUCKINGHAM PALACE, 1913'
SIR JOHN LAVERY, 1913

Oil on canvas, 3403 x 2718mm
NPG 1745

CONTENTS

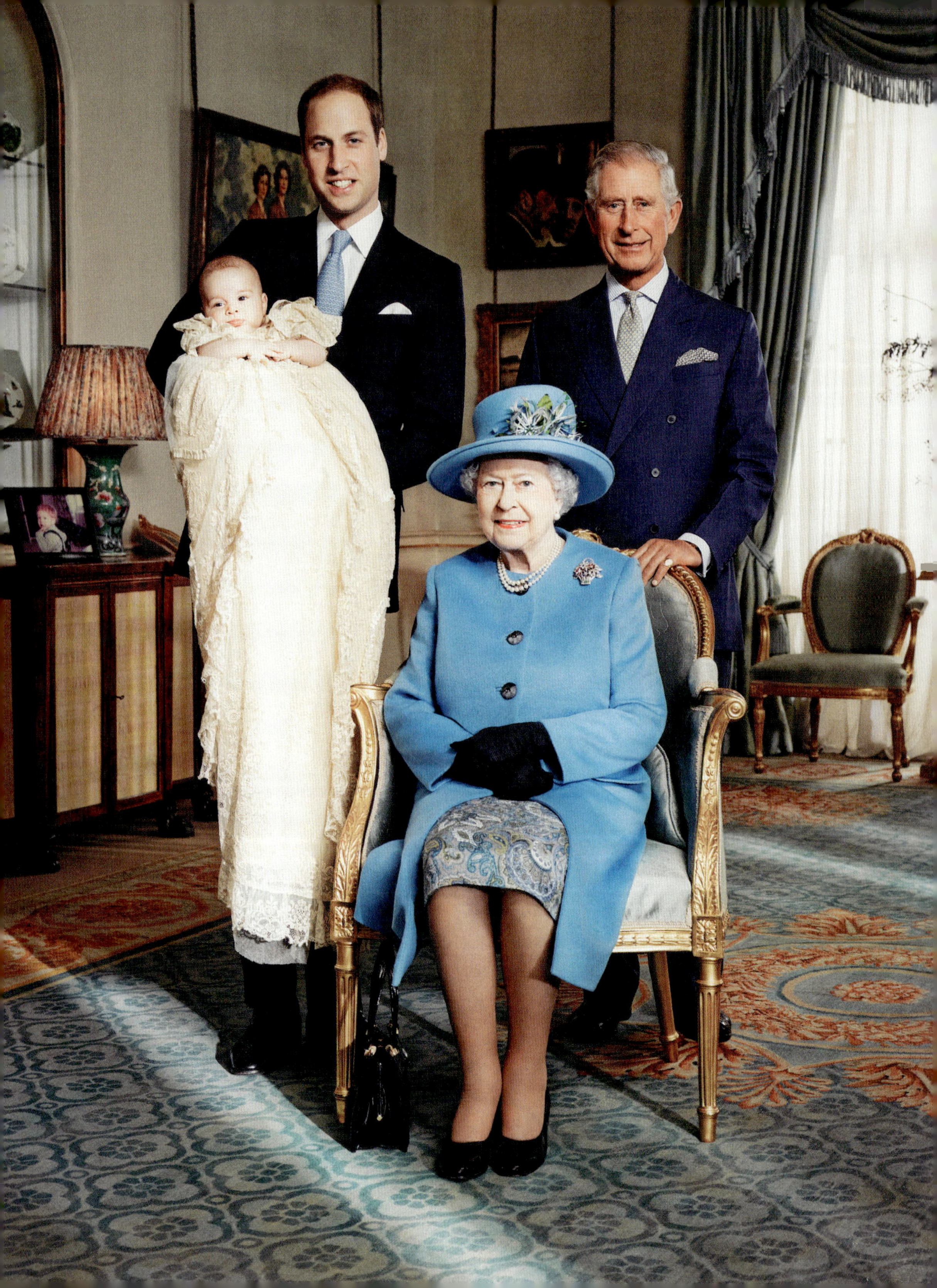

POWER AND THE CROWN

Rab MacGibbon

Monarchy, meaning 'the rule of one', concentrates the power to govern a nation into the hands of a single individual. It has been the most common system of government throughout world history. Within the British Isles, kings and queens have reigned for over two millennia. Monarchs have exercised absolute power and changed the political and religious course of the entire population. In other periods, and increasingly over time, monarchs have wielded less executive power while retaining a significant role as national figureheads.

The long history of the monarchy was ever present during the spectacular coronation of King Charles III at Westminster Abbey on 6 May 2023. His ceremonial crowning as sovereign of the United Kingdom followed a centuries-old ritual. The King's anointment with holy oil, giving his reign divine sanction, has its origins in the Bible. The magnificent setting and historic regalia presented the King's accession as the natural evolution of an ancient lineage. The strength of the royal tradition had been reinforced by the 70-year reign of his unceasingly dutiful and much-admired mother, Queen Elizabeth II. The meticulously staged event celebrated what is regarded as one of the principal strengths of a hereditary monarchy – the stable and orderly transition from one ruler to the next. In this respect, the House of Windsor is in an exceptionally robust position with a clearly established line of succession over the next two generations. This is the subject of Jason Bell's photograph of four generations of the royal line of succession, taken to mark the christening of Prince George in 2013 (fig.1).

While royal image makers and regal pomp and ceremony promote a reassuring narrative of constancy and continuity, the very crown at the heart of the coronation service tells an alternative story of instability and rupture. It is named St Edward's Crown after

[FIG.1]
PRINCE GEORGE OF WALES, WILLIAM, THE PRINCE OF WALES, QUEEN ELIZABETH II AND KING CHARLES III
(b.2013; b.1982; 1926–2022; b.1948)
JASON BELL, 23 OCTOBER 2013

Archival inkjet print, 525 x 405mm
NPG x138989

King Edward 'the Confessor', who founded, and is buried in, Westminster Abbey and became the patron saint of the royal family. However, Edward's failure to effectively manage the succession resulted in the Norman invasion, which violently ended the Anglo-Saxon line of kings. The first coronation in Westminster Abbey using St Edward's Crown was for the conquering King William I, from whom all subsequent monarchs of England are ultimately descended. The second great crisis evidenced by the crown was the country's descent into civil war in the seventeenth century, which resulted in the execution of King Charles I, the establishment of a republic and the destruction of the crown jewels. King Charles III's coronation crown was therefore not that worn by Edward the Confessor but a replacement made for King Charles II after the collapse of the republic and the restoration of the monarchy in 1660. The crown can therefore be regarded as much as a symbol of the monarchy's ability to adapt and survive as of its long-established tradition.

A book such as this can only tell a partial story of the monarchy. Missing from its pages are the ancient and medieval rulers over shifting regions of the British Isles. Even once these smaller kingdoms had broadly consolidated into today's England, Scotland, Wales, Ireland and Northern Ireland, only those monarchs who wore the English crown are included. This is primarily because the English monarchs form the direct line of succession to today's royal family. The political and dynastic fluctuations of the shared history of these islands means that a focus on the monarchy in England does not exclude the other nations. Ireland joins the story with the creation of the title of King of Ireland for Henry VIII of England in 1542. Four centuries later the majority of the island rejected the monarchy with the establishment of the Republic of Ireland in 1949. Likewise Scotland, whose monarchy predates that of England, enters the narrative with the accession of King James VI of Scotland as James I of England and Ireland in 1603. Wales is present primarily through the title of Prince of Wales, which has been held by the heirs to the English throne since the conquest of Wales by King Edward I in 1283.

Two centuries later the Welsh Tudor family won the English crown in dramatic fashion when Henry Tudor defeated King Richard III at the Battle of Bosworth in 1485. It is only from this moment of violent regime change that the National Portrait Gallery's history of the monarchy can begin. This is because the earliest painted portrait in the Collection depicts King Henry VII in 1505, 20 years after he seized the crown (p.21). Few earlier monarchs ever sat for their portrait and the Gallery's aim to present notable figures with authentic, lifetime portraits means that it is only possible to do justice to the last five centuries of our history. British portraits painted earlier than 1500 are scarce and it was only under the Tudors that a fully developed portrait culture emerged. This flourishing was influenced by humanist ideas from continental Europe, where a renewed emphasis on individual identity meant that portraits became highly valued. The specific context of the Tudors was also a factor, in which portraiture became a crucial tool in bolstering their fragile claim to legitimacy through symbolic displays of royal power and authority. Under the Tudors, portraits of earlier monarchs were also made to visually reinforce the dynasty's place in the line of succession. Numerous depictions of King Richard III were made with the differing aim of undermining the moral and legal authority of the king that the Tudors had deposed (fig.2).

Within hereditary monarchies, the dynastic imperative of producing heirs is of no less importance than the sovereign's governance of the kingdom and command of the armed forces. The struggle for a legitimate male heir became the overriding focus of the reign of the succeeding Tudor monarch, King Henry VIII, with profound and unexpected consequences for the nation. The king attempted to terminate his marriage to Katherine of Aragon once it became apparent that Princess Mary would be their only child. The pope's refusal to annul the marriage led to England's break with the Roman Catholic Church. As head of a newly established Protestant Church of England as well as being king, Henry centralised the crown's power, wealth and authority to an unprecedented level. The second of his six marriages, to Anne Boleyn, produced Princess Elizabeth, but the lack of a male heir saw her ousted and eventually beheaded. His third wife, Jane Seymour, died shortly after giving birth to Henry's longed-for male heir, Prince Edward. A rare, symbolic depiction of the process of succession shows Henry VIII on his deathbed pointing to his nine-year-old son and heir Edward VI (fig.3). The event is overseen by members of his council while scenes of religious iconoclasm take place outside and a pope is crushed by the Protestant 'word of the Lord'. In the end, Henry VIII's hopes for a long and stable dynasty were dashed, as none of his three children to ascend the throne – Edward, Mary or Elizabeth – produced an heir to continue the line.

A recurrent feature of the monarchy's resilience had been its ability to incorporate new bloodlines when necessary or expedient. Strict rules of

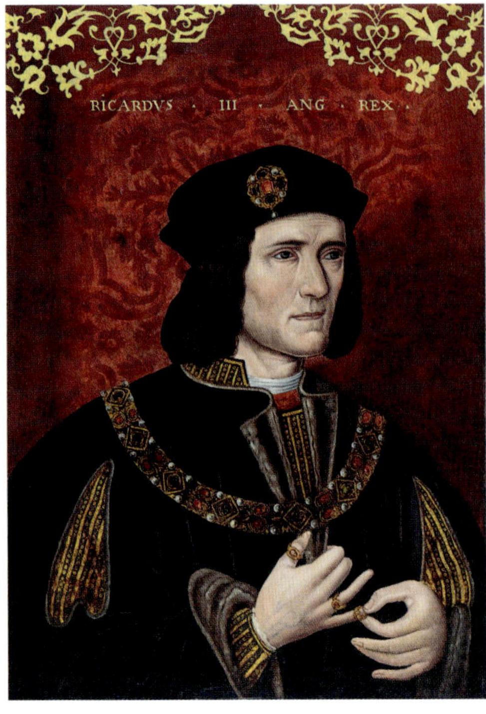

[FIG.2]
KING RICHARD III
(1452–85)
UNKNOWN ARTIST, LATE 16th CENTURY

Oil on panel, 638 x 470mm
NPG 148

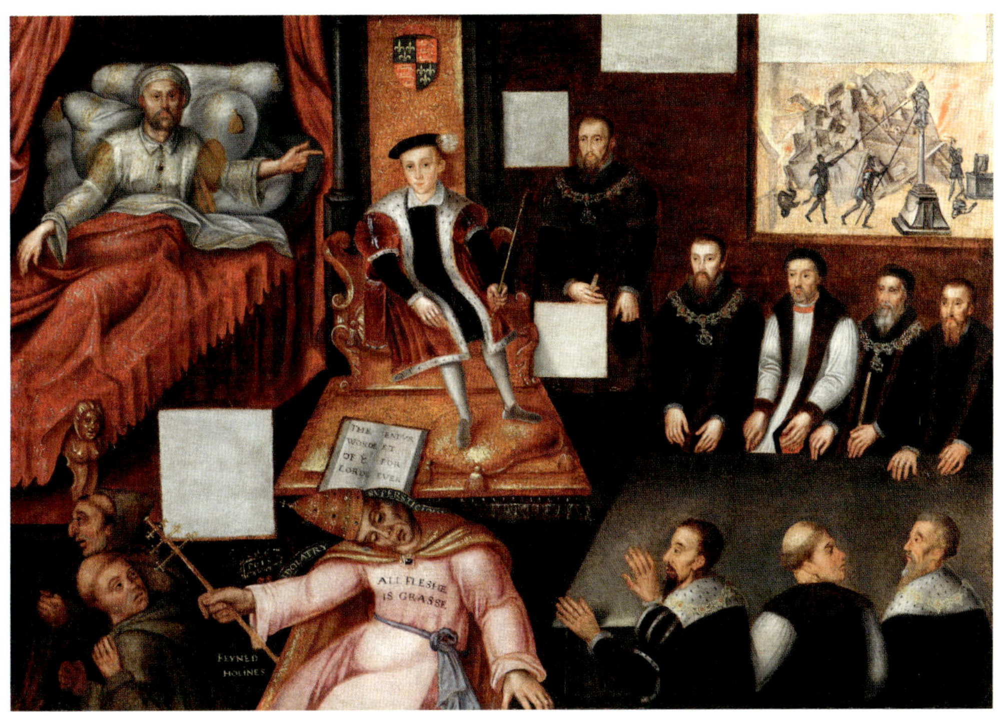

[FIG.3]
KING EDWARD VI AND THE POPE
KING HENRY VIII (1491–1547) AND KING EDWARD VI (1537–53)
UNKNOWN ARTIST, c.1575

Oil on panel, 622 x 908mm
NPG 4165

hereditary succession have been overruled and even recent adversaries have been offered the crown. Queen Elizabeth I was succeeded by her cousin James VI of Scotland, whose mother, Mary, Queen of Scots, had been executed on Elizabeth's orders. The transition to the Stuart dynasty was nevertheless remarkably smooth, and under James, the crowns of England and Scotland were united.

The Stuart dynasty experienced the most traumatic interruption to the rules of hereditary monarchy in British history. A civil war between Charles I and Parliament resulted in the king's death in 1649. He is the only British monarch to have been tried and executed by his subjects (fig.4). Following the restoration of the Stuart monarchy in 1660, after Parliament failed to establish a republic, the later years of the dynasty were characterised by a similar flexibility about the rules of hereditary succession with which it began. In 1688, the Protestant Dutch ruler, William of Orange, was invited to invade, depose the Catholic King James II and rule in a joint monarchy with his wife Mary, James's daughter. Their reign marked the beginning of Britain's constitutional monarchy, whereby the sovereign's power diminished as that of Parliament increased.

The 1701 Act of Settlement, which ensured a Protestant succession to the throne, laid the path for the second incorporation of a royal family from overseas. When the last Stuart monarch, the childless Queen Anne, died in 1714, her distant cousin, George of Hanover, inherited the throne in favour of dozens of closer Catholic relatives. Though he spoke little English and spent much of his time in Germany, King George I reigned over a new Kingdom of Great Britain, which had been created through the 1707 Act of Union between England and Scotland. Dynastically, the House of Hanover was characterised by tensions between the monarch and heir. The contrast between the personal restraint of King George III and his self-indulgent son, the future King George IV, was the subject of biting satires (fig.5). Such public ridicule would have been unthinkable in earlier eras and is evidence of the monarchy's reduced authority during a period of evolving parliamentary democracy.

The right of parliamentary legislation to override hereditary succession did not go unchallenged. Catholic Stuart claimants to the throne led uprisings in 1715 and 1745 and were only finally defeated at

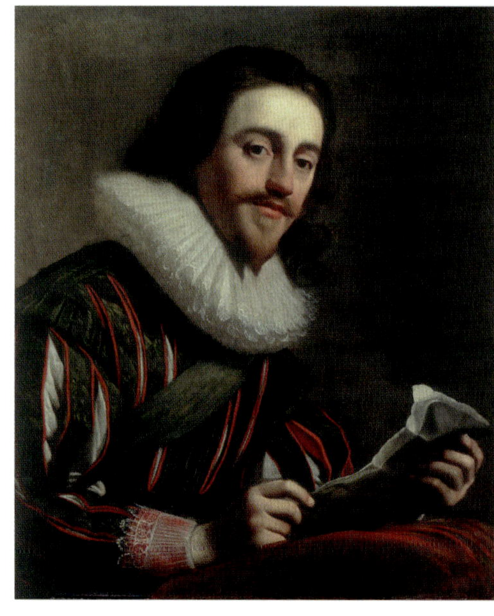

[FIG.4]
KING CHARLES I
(1600–49)
GERRIT VAN HONTHORST, 1628

Oil on canvas, 762 x 641mm
NPG 4444

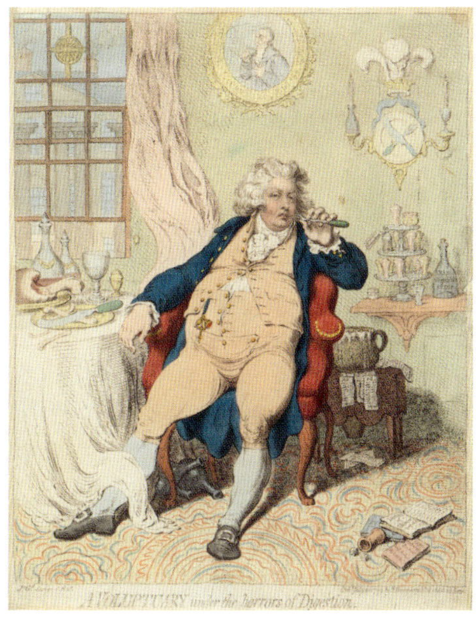

[FIG.5]
'A VOLUPTUARY UNDER THE HORRORS OF DIGESTION'
KING GEORGE IV (1762–1830)
JAMES GILLRAY, PUBLISHED BY HANNAH HUMPHREY, 2 JULY 1792

Hand-coloured stipple, 363 x 290mm
NPG D12460

the Battle of Culloden in 1746. The succession of four kings named George means that this period of the Hanoverian dynasty is often referred to as the Georgian era. While Queen Victoria was no less a member of this dynasty than her male predecessors, her reign was of such length and so distinctive in character, that she is usually considered in isolation from them. Her 63-year reign is characterised by the growth of Britain's economic and military power. Britain's colonial territories, which began with Tudor settlements and conquests, developed into an empire.

The height of Britain's imperial era lasted from Parliament's declaration of Victoria as Empress of India in 1876 until India achieved independence in 1947. Even at the head of a global empire, the monarchy's political power further retreated through the expansion of democratic and social rights in Britain during this period. Its symbolic role as a focus of national identity and belonging was instead enhanced through the royal pomp and magnificence of coronations, weddings and jubilees. Indeed, the British monarchy's relative political weakness can be regarded as a fundamental strength of the institution.

Beginning with the French Revolution in 1789 through to the collapse of the German and Russian monarchies in the wake of the First World War, the European monarchs that attempted to resist societal change and cling on to executive power were deposed. In contrast, King George V and his descendants focused the monarchy's efforts on demonstrations of public service and duty. The British monarchy's talent for survival was shown in 1917 when, in light of anti-German feeling during the war, George V changed the family's name from Saxe-Coburg and Gotha (the surname of Victoria's German husband, Prince Albert), to the more patriotic sounding Windsor, after their oldest and most iconic residence. While the Windsors have retained an important role in government – for instance no parliamentary bill can be passed into law until it has received royal assent – they have embraced their principal role as national figureheads.

In the twentieth century, the House of Windsor was tested by the abdication crisis of King Edward VIII in 1936, the decline in social deference and the intensification of scrutiny and media intrusion. The end of the British Empire provided the opportunity to establish a more equitable association of independent countries around the globe, almost all of which were formerly part of the Empire. The sovereign would no longer rule as emperor, but as Head of the Commonwealth they would remain the ceremonial leader of almost a third of the world population.

In the twenty-first century, Queen Elizabeth II was widely regarded as exemplifying the monarch's role as a focus for national identity and unity, especially at a time of widespread societal and political discord. Her sense of duty is equally present in her heirs, as evidenced by the charitable and military service of her children and grandchildren, including Prince William and Prince Harry, who were painted by Nicky Philipps in their uniforms as officers of the Household Cavalry (Blues and Royals) (fig.6). As constitutional monarchs, the Windsors know that they rule by consent. In a modern, democratic and multicultural society with a rich diversity of social, political and religious beliefs, the hierarchy and values enshrined in the monarchy will be scrutinised and debated. Under King Charles III and his successors, the monarchy will continue to adapt and evolve, as has always been the case, even while it projects a vision of tradition and permanence.

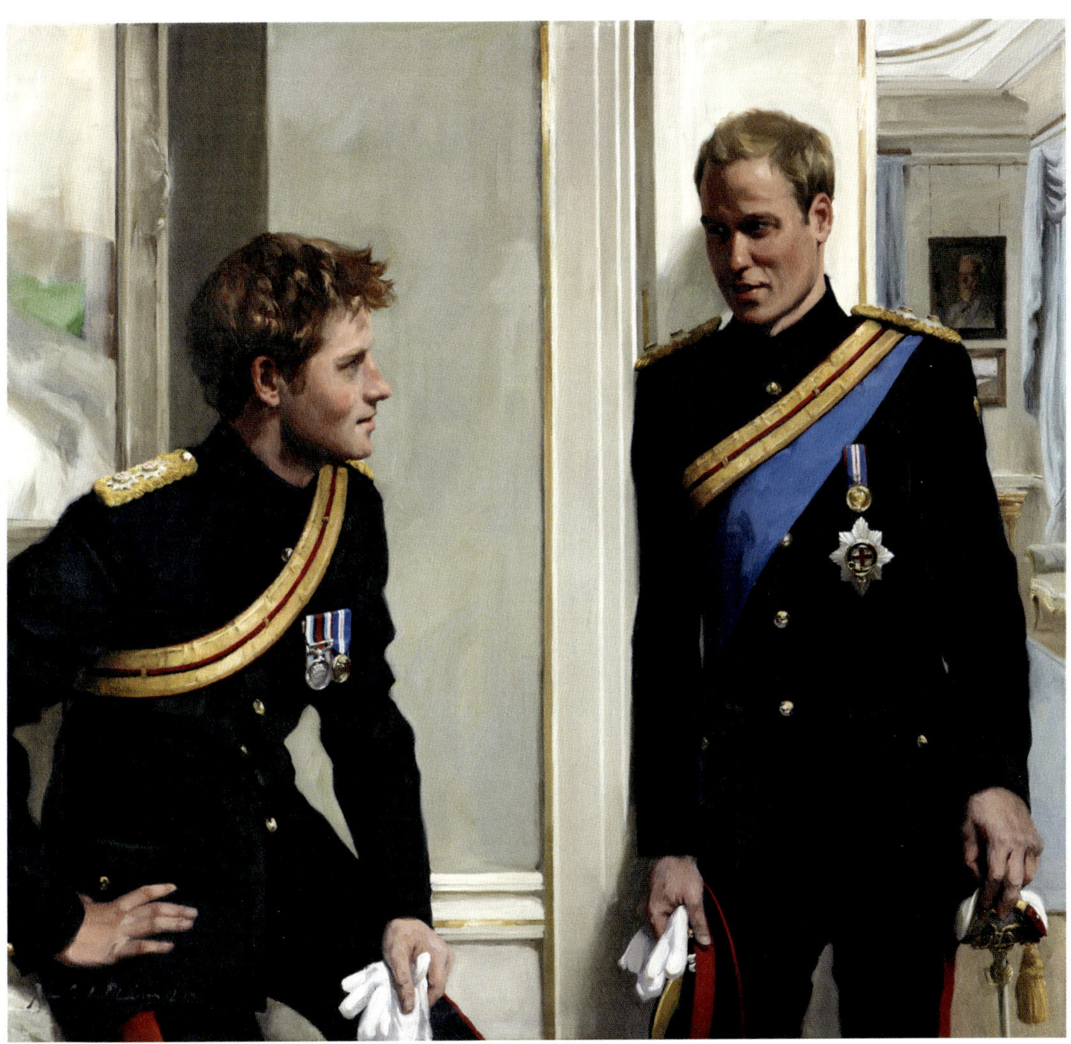

[FIG.6]
PRINCE HARRY, DUKE OF SUSSEX AND WILLIAM, THE PRINCE OF WALES
(b.1984; b.1982)
NICKY PHILIPPS, 2009

Oil on canvas, 1374 x 1475mm
NPG 6876

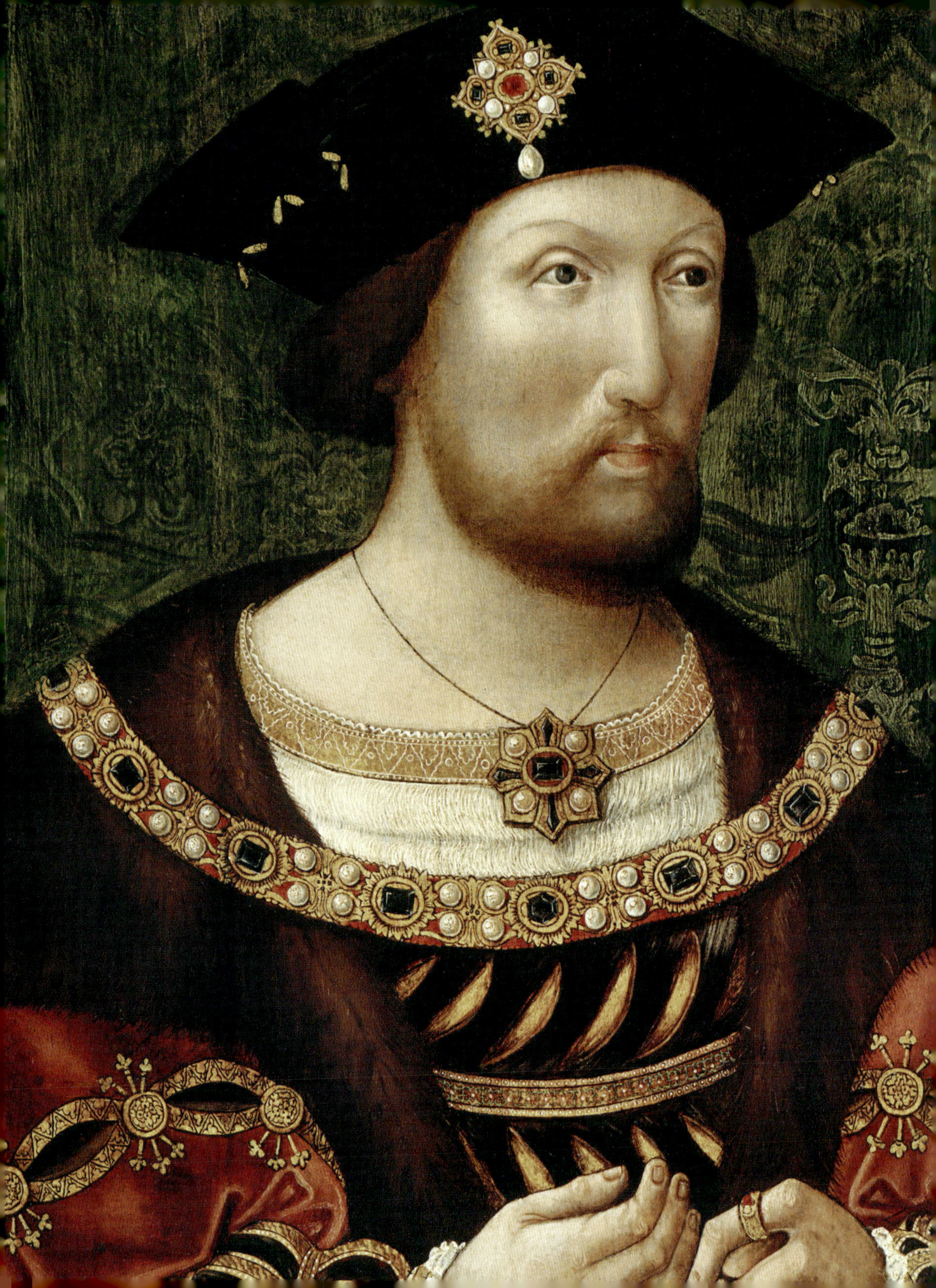

THE TUDORS

1485–1603

Previous spread (detail)
KING HENRY VIII
UNKNOWN ARTIST, c.1520

Oil on panel, 508 x 381mm
NPG 4690

The Tudors are perhaps the most famous dynasty to have ruled within the British Isles. They were immortalised in portraiture and then written into history in chronicles and plays, before evolving into characters of fiction on the page and screen.

The first Tudor king, Henry VII, seized the throne from Richard III at the Battle of Bosworth in 1485. Henry's victory ended a period of civil conflict that has come to be known as the Wars of the Roses (1455–87).

Henry VII was succeeded by his second son, Henry VIII, whose first act as king was to marry his brother's widow, the Spanish princess Katherine of Aragon. In pursuit of a legitimate male heir, and in order to marry Anne Boleyn, Henry reshaped the power structures of the nation in establishing the Church of England.

Henry's execution of Anne set him on a path to marital notoriety. His third wife, Jane Seymour, died shortly after giving birth to Prince Edward in 1537, and Henry went on to marry Anne of Cleves, Katherine Howard and Katherine Parr in quick succession.

Edward VI was only 9 years old when he acceded the throne, and his early death resulted in the nine-day reign of Lady Jane Grey and the accession of England's first queen regnant, Mary I. Mary died childless in 1558, ensuring the succession of her Protestant half-sister Elizabeth I. Elizabeth was 25 years old when she became queen, and went on to rule for over 40 years. Religious divisions in the country meant that Elizabeth's position was threatened by her Roman Catholic cousin, Mary, Queen of Scots, until the Scottish queen's execution in 1587. Elizabeth's death in 1603 brought an end to the Tudor dynasty.

Henry Tudor had a tenuous claim to the English throne through his mother's descent from Edward III. Skilful and shrewd, Henry defeated Richard III at the Battle of Bosworth and on the battlefield was crowned King Henry VII (r.1485–1509).

The victory brought about peace and prosperity after 30 years of civil strife. Through taxation, treaties and trade promotion, Henry amassed enormous wealth for the crown.

Henry's cleverly orchestrated marriage to Elizabeth of York, the daughter of Edward IV, united the red rose of Lancaster and the white rose of York, founding a family that would rule England and Wales for three generations under the emblem of the red and white Tudor rose.

This is the earliest painted portrait in the National Portrait Gallery's Collection. The inscription records that it was painted on 29 October 1505. The portrait was sent to Margaret of Austria as part of negotiations when Henry was looking to remarry following Elizabeth's death in 1503.

[1]
KING HENRY VII
(1457–1509)
UNKNOWN ARTIST, 1505

Oil on panel, 425 x 305mm
NPG 416

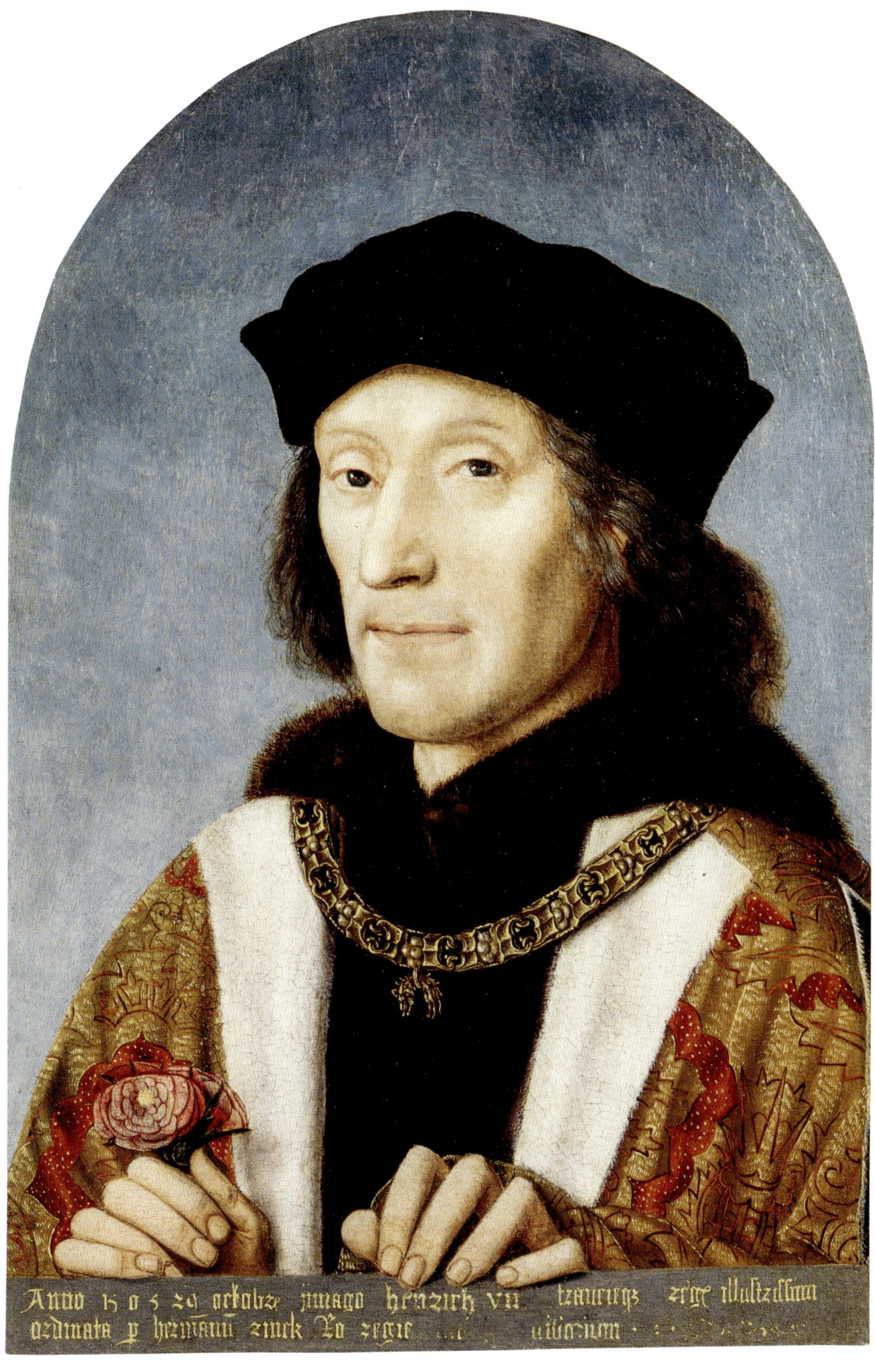

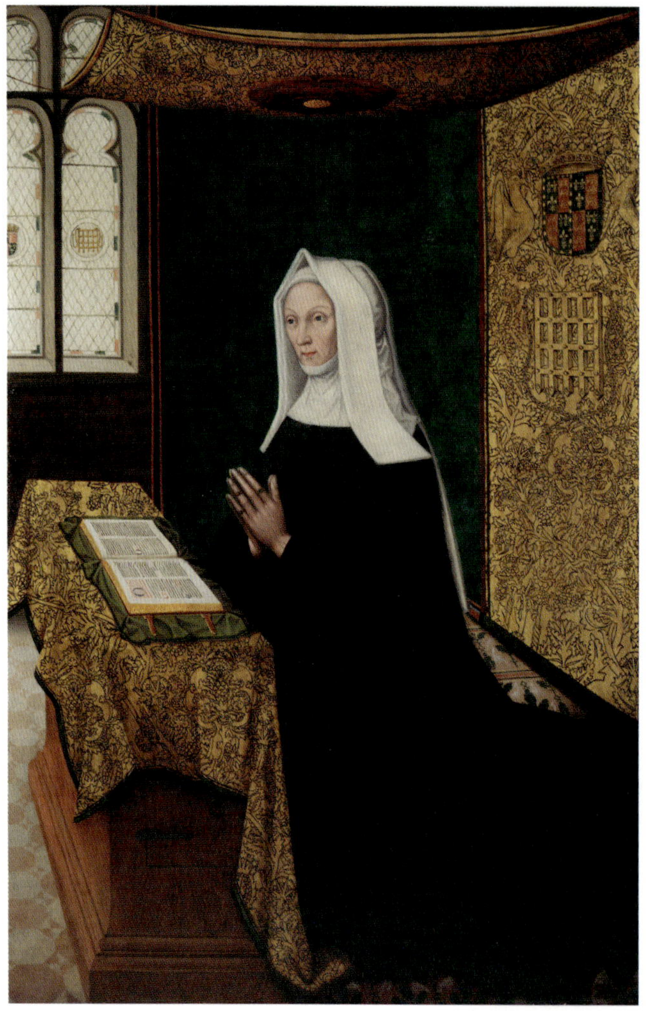

Lady Margaret Beaufort was only 13 when she gave birth to the future Henry VII in 1457. As a descendent of Edward III, Lady Margaret's lineage was the basis of Henry's claim to the throne. She played a decisive role in his rise to power, including negotiating his marriage to Elizabeth of York.

Once Henry became king, Lady Margaret set up her own magnificent household. She was an active religious and educational patron, founding St John's College and Christ's College at the University of Cambridge.

[2]
LADY MARGARET BEAUFORT, COUNTESS OF RICHMOND AND DERBY
(1443–1509)
MEYNNART WEWYCK, c.1510

Oil on panel, 1800 x 1220mm
NPG L270

Henry VII's marriage to Elizabeth of York, the daughter of the Yorkist king, Edward IV, helped to bring an end to the Wars of the Roses. With opposition to the Tudor dynasty appeased, public acceptance of the new reign was widespread.

Elizabeth can be seen here holding the white rose, a symbol of the House of York. Portraits from the period frequently depict Henry holding the red rose of the House of Lancaster. Their two emblems fused to create the red and white Tudor rose.

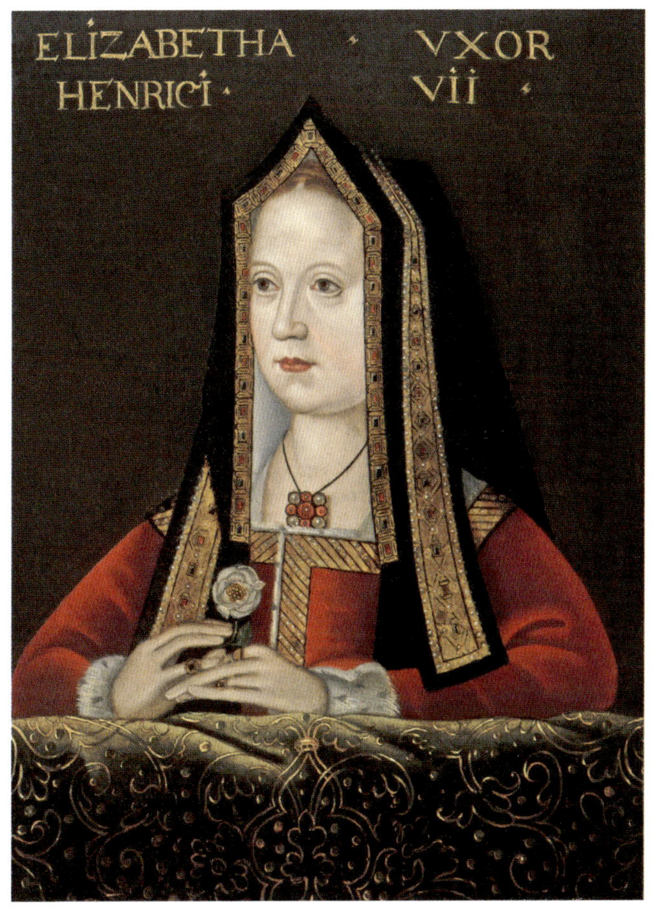

[3]
ELIZABETH OF YORK
(1466–1503)
UNKNOWN ARTIST, LATE 16th CENTURY, BASED ON A WORK OF c.1500

Oil on panel, 565 x 416mm
NPG 311

As second son, Henry was not expected to rule. However, the death of his older brother, Arthur, Prince of Wales, in 1502, changed his fate. Shortly before Henry's 18th birthday, he acceded the throne, becoming King Henry VIII (r.1509–47).

Perhaps most widely known for his six marriages in pursuit of a legitimate male heir, Henry's reign was characterised by ambition abroad and ruthlessness at home. He initiated the break from the Catholic Church in Rome and appointed himself Supreme Head of the Church in England. Henry transferred the Church's assets to the Crown and nobility following the dissolution of the religious houses in England. This granted the monarch greater personal power than at any previous point in history.

[4]
KING HENRY VIII
(1491–1547)
AFTER HANS HOLBEIN THE YOUNGER, PROBABLY 17th CENTURY, BASED ON A WORK OF 1536

Oil on copper, 279 x 200mm
NPG 157

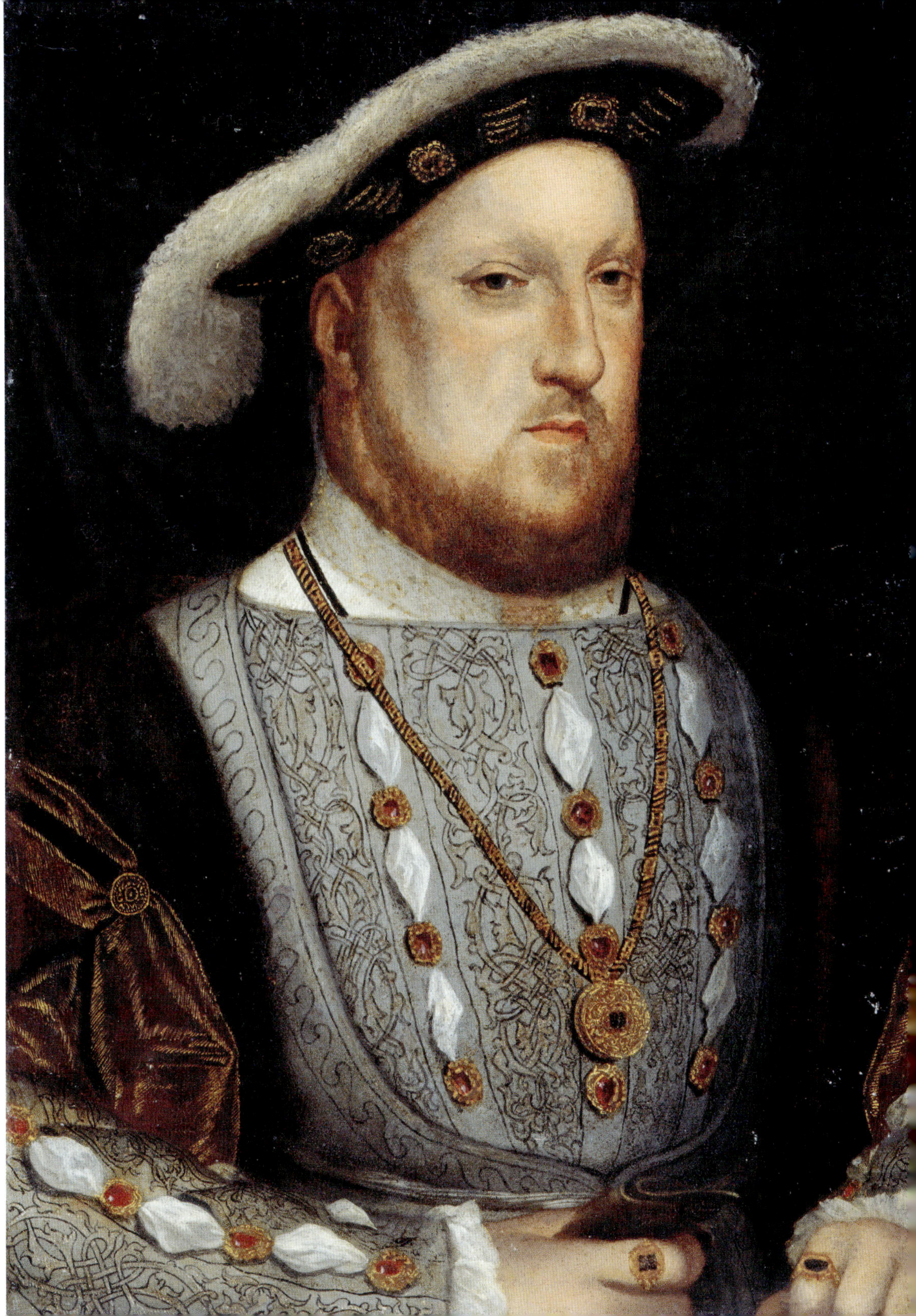

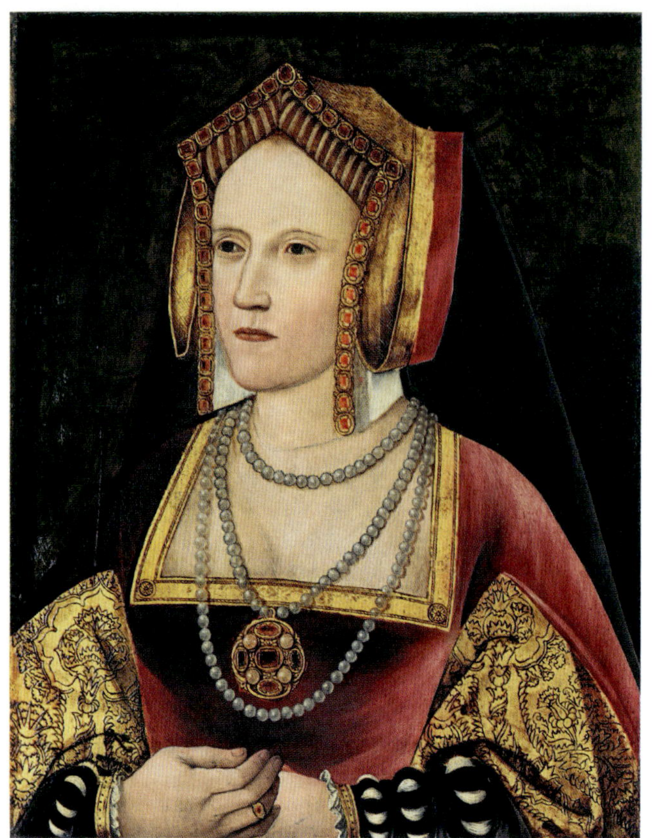

Katherine of Aragon was the daughter of Ferdinand of Aragon and Isabella of Castile. She came to England in 1501 to marry Prince Arthur. Seven years after Arthur's sudden death, Katherine married his brother Henry VIII.

Henry and Katherine were jointly crowned in 1509; however, following many miscarriages and the death of their son, Henry, at seven weeks old, the dynastic imperative to produce a legitimate male heir spurred Henry to disavow his wife. In 1533, Katherine's 23-year marriage to Henry was annulled, on the grounds that Henry could not marry his brother's widow.

This portrait was probably intended to be paired with an image of Henry. Katherine never accepted the annulment of her marriage or the title Princess Dowager of Wales, and, poignantly, paired portraits were listed in the inventory of her possessions taken after her death.

[5]
KATHERINE OF ARAGON
(1485–1536)
UNKNOWN ARTIST, c.1520

Oil on panel, 520 x 420mm
NPG L246

Anne Boleyn had been courted by Henry VIII for years but refused to become his mistress. She finally married Henry in secret in 1533, before his first marriage had been annulled, giving birth to a daughter, Elizabeth, later that year.

Anne was committed to the cause of religious reform but clashed with Thomas Cromwell, the king's chief minister. Without a son, her status in the king's eyes diminished and Cromwell moved against her, raising suspicions that she had committed adultery. Anne was found guilty of treason and executed in 1536.

No contemporary painting of Anne survives. It is possible that images of her were deliberately destroyed, in the same way that her heraldic devices were removed from the royal palaces after her execution. However, her reputation and image enjoyed a resurgence during the long reign of her daughter, Elizabeth I.

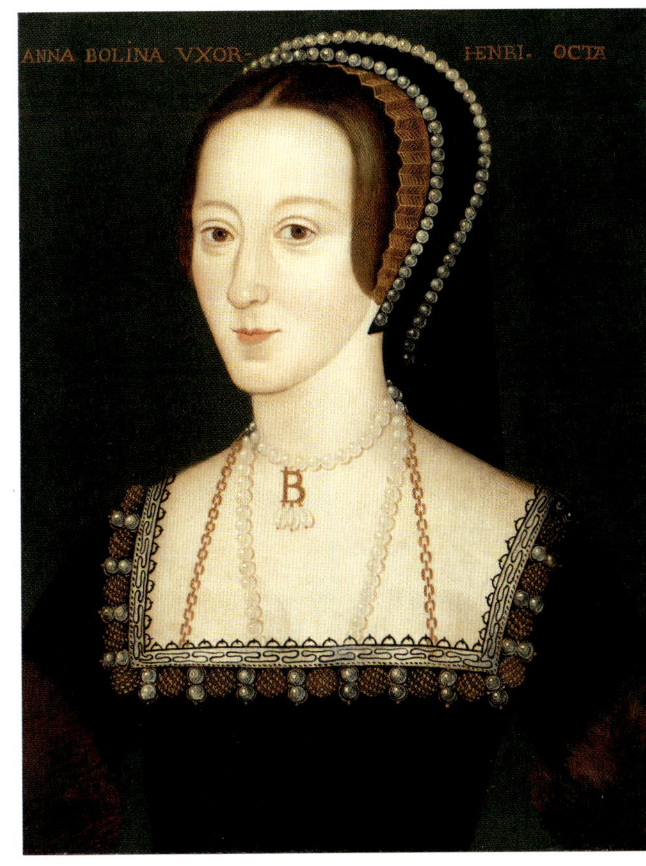

[6]
ANNE BOLEYN
(*c*.1500–36)
UNKNOWN ARTIST, LATE 16th CENTURY

Oil on panel, 543 x 416mm
NPG 668

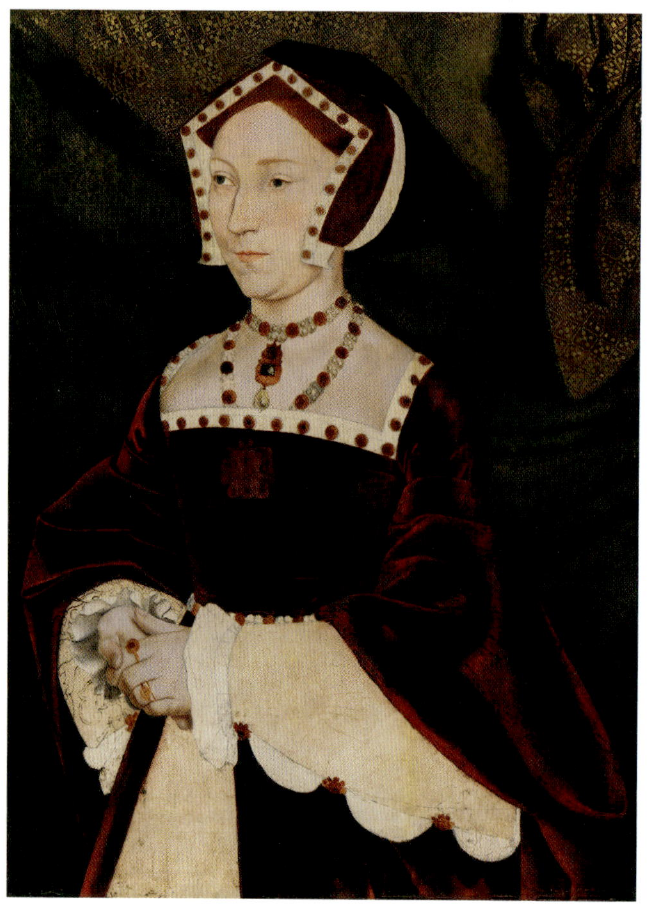

Jane Seymour was formally betrothed to Henry VIII the day after Anne Boleyn's execution in 1536. She gave birth to a son, Edward, the following year. However, childbirth was fraught with danger at the time, and Jane died less than a fortnight later, leaving Henry to lament that 'Divine Providence has mingled my joy with the bitterness of the death of her who brought me this happiness'.

This portrait is unfinished, awaiting layers of silver and gold leaf to complete the decoration. It may have been abandoned at Holbein's death in 1543 during an outbreak of plague, or, if commissioned by one of Jane's brothers, after their downfall during the reign of Edward VI.

[7]
JANE SEYMOUR
(1508/9–37)
STUDIO OF HANS HOLBEIN THE YOUNGER, *c.*1537

Oil on panel, 640 x 480mm
NPG 7025

Anne of Cleves became Henry VIII's fourth wife a little over two years after Jane Seymour's death. The marriage was negotiated by Thomas Cromwell, who viewed it as a means to bolster Henry's commitment to religious reform. Upon her arrival Henry complained that Anne did not look like the portrait he was initially shown. The marriage was never consummated, which gave legal grounds for its annulment.

Anne was treated well by the king following their divorce and she retained her royal status. She received a generous income and was in attendance at Mary I's coronation. The last survivor of Henry's wives, Anne died in 1557, and was buried in Westminster Abbey.

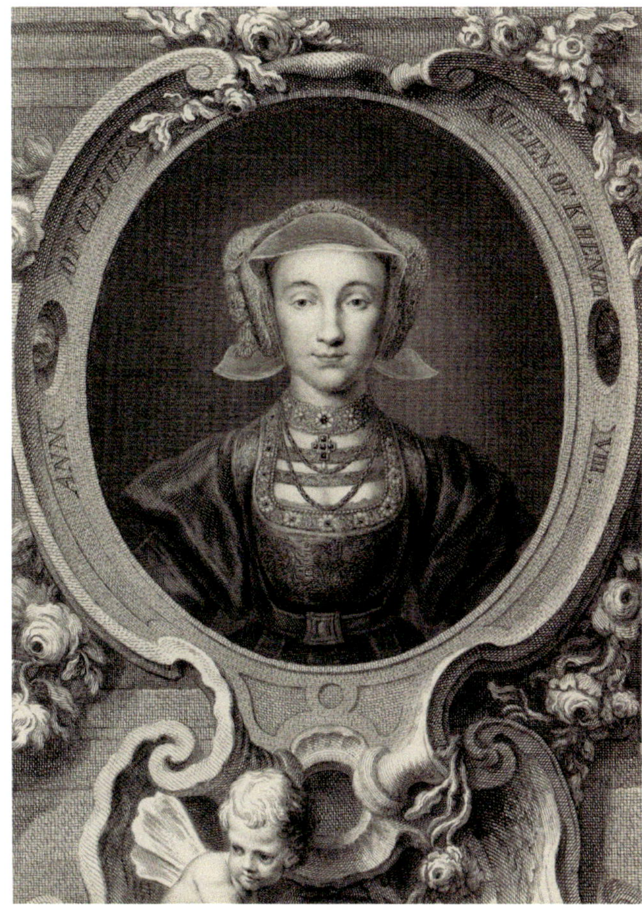

[8]
ANNE OF CLEVES
(1515–57)
JACOBUS HOUBRAKEN, AFTER HANS HOLBEIN THE YOUNGER, 1739

Engraving, 286 x 207mm
NPG D9087

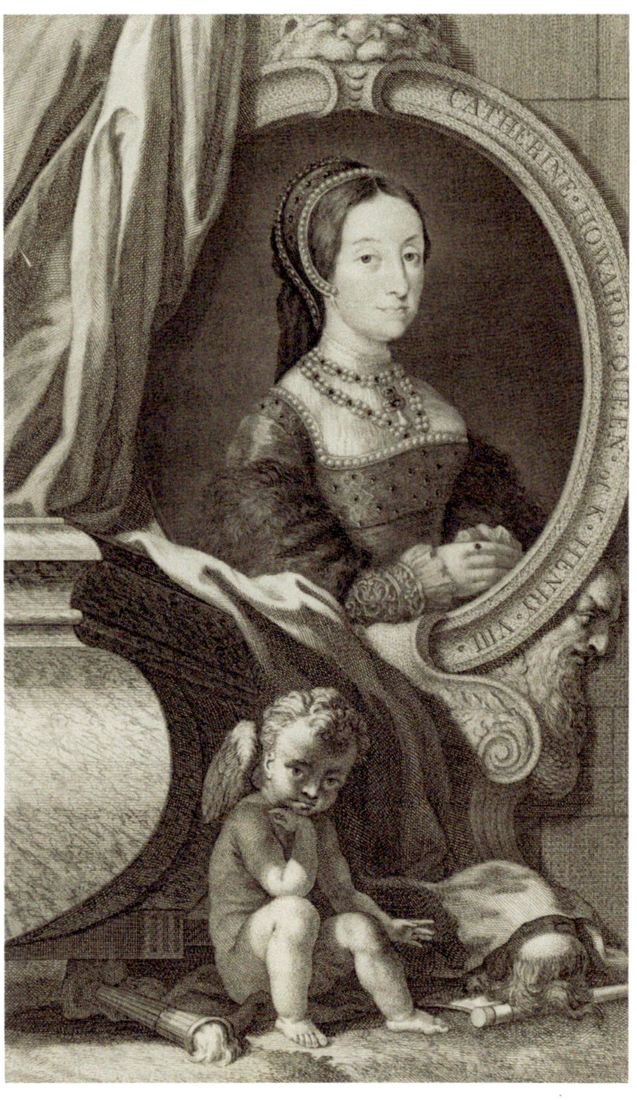

A first cousin of Anne Boleyn, Katherine Howard married Henry VIII on 28 July 1540. Thomas Cromwell, the architect of the king's fourth marriage, was executed at the Tower on the same day. Henry was besotted with Katherine, prompting the French ambassador to report that 'he cannot treat her well enough and caresses her more than he did the others'.

Katherine's downfall was as rapid as her ascent. It was reported to Henry that she had concealed information about her prior relationships with men. During investigations into whether these relationships had continued after her marriage, it was found that she had intended to commit adultery. Katherine was executed in 1542 and buried near to Anne Boleyn.

[9]
POSSIBLY KATHERINE HOWARD
(c.1518–42)
JACOBUS HOUBRAKEN, AFTER HANS HOLBEIN THE YOUNGER, 1730s

Engraving, 550 x 400mm
NPG D42876

The sixth and last wife of Henry VIII, Katherine Parr married the king at Hampton Court on 12 July 1543. The following year, she was appointed Governor and Protector of the Realm when Henry renewed war with France and was absent from England for two months.

Katherine used her position as queen consort to promote religious reform, becoming the first English woman to publish books in her own name.

After the king's death, Katherine married Sir Thomas Seymour, Baron Seymour of Sudeley (Jane Seymour's brother), but died a year later, shortly after giving birth to a daughter.

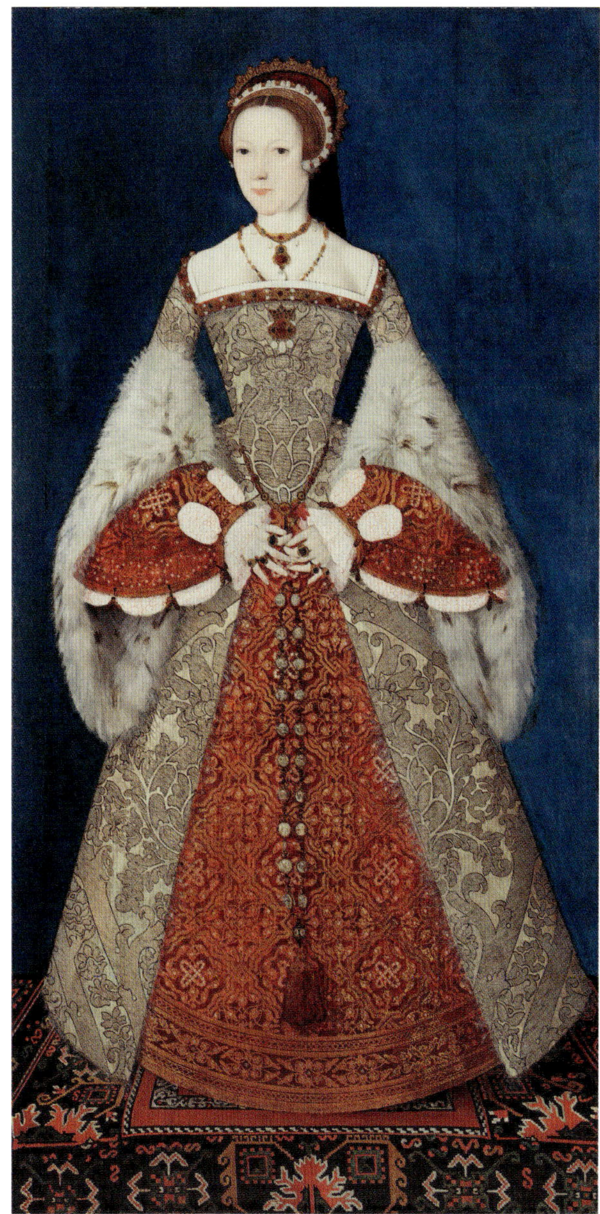

[10]
KATHERINE PARR
(1512–48)
UNKNOWN ARTIST, c.1543

Oil on panel, 1803 x 940mm
NPG 4451

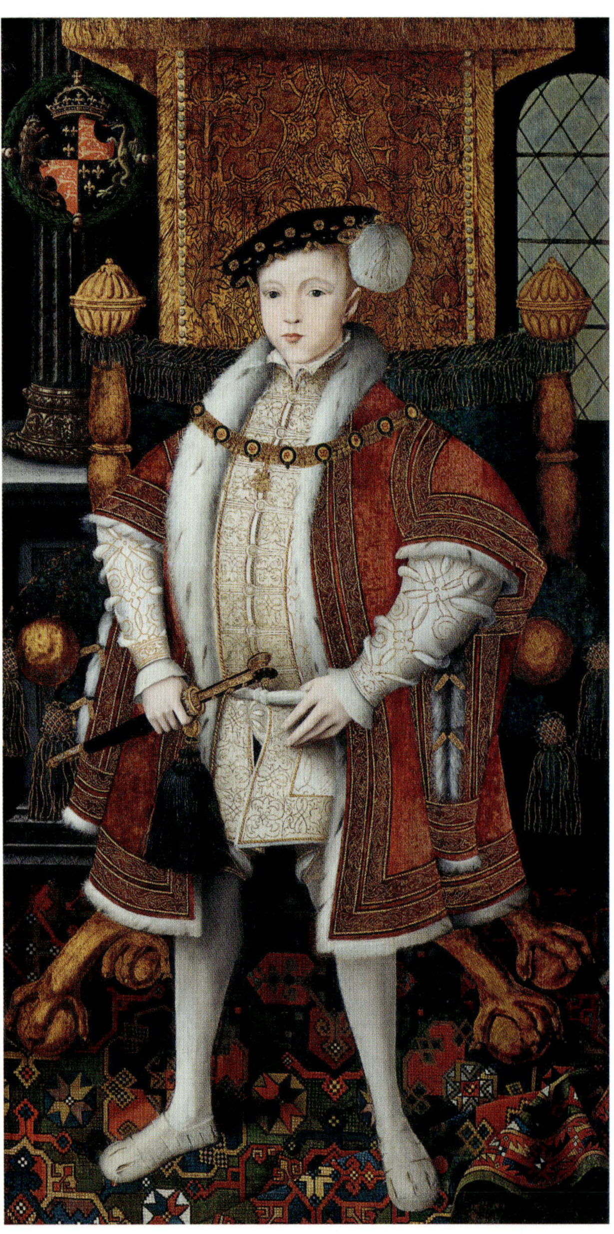

Edward was born to Henry VIII and Jane Seymour, Henry's third wife, in 1537. Jane died 12 days after giving birth. Although Edward was only nine years old when he became King Edward VI (r.1547–53), his reign, under the stewardship of his uncle Edward Seymour, Duke of Somerset, and subsequently John Dudley, Duke of Northumberland, saw the establishment of Protestantism across the country.

Anxious about his Catholic half-sister Mary taking the throne, Edward attempted to secure the Protestant succession by naming his cousin, Lady Jane Grey, as his heir. He died, probably from tuberculosis, aged only 15.

As heir to the throne, Edward was painted a number of times throughout his childhood. This portrait was painted for his investiture as Prince of Wales, but was transformed into a representation of Edward as king after his father's death, through the inclusion of the royal coat of arms.

[11]
KING EDWARD VI
(1537–53)
UNKNOWN ARTIST, c.1547

Oil on panel, 1556 x 813mm
NPG 5511

Lady Jane Grey (r.1553) was the granddaughter of Henry VIII's youngest sister, Mary Tudor. Edward VI named Jane his successor in order to block the accession of his Catholic half-sister, Mary. However, Mary had enough support to claim the throne less than a fortnight after Edward's death. Jane was sent to the Tower of London and condemned for treason. Jane's life was initially spared, but her father's involvement in Sir Thomas Wyatt's rebellion in 1554 sealed her fate.

It is possible that a portrait of Jane was never made during her lifetime and almost certain that no image of her was made during her very brief period as queen. This image was probably produced in response to Jane's growing reputation as a Protestant martyr during Elizabeth I's reign; the scratched lines across the eyes and mouth appear to be the result of a deliberate attack at some point in its history.

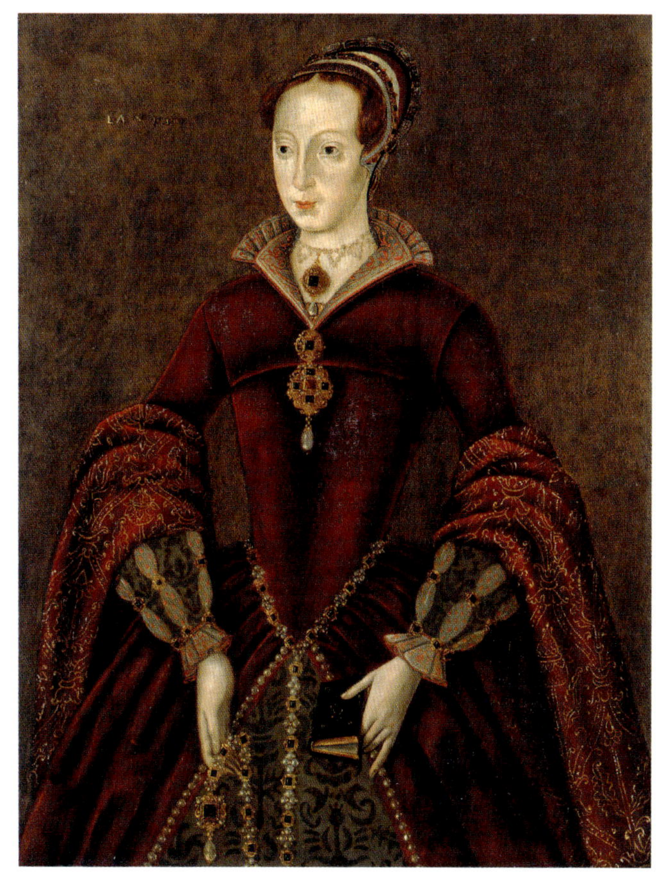

[12]
LADY JANE GREY
(1537–54)
UNKNOWN ARTIST, c.1590–1600

Oil on oak panel, 856 x 603mm
NPG 6804

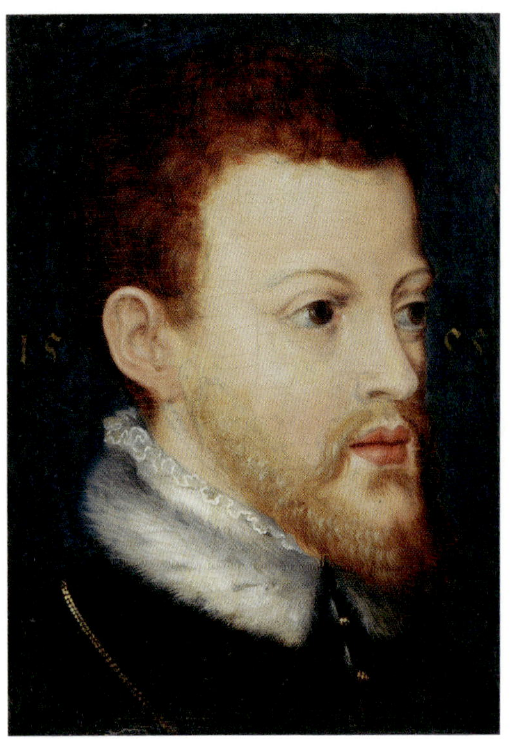

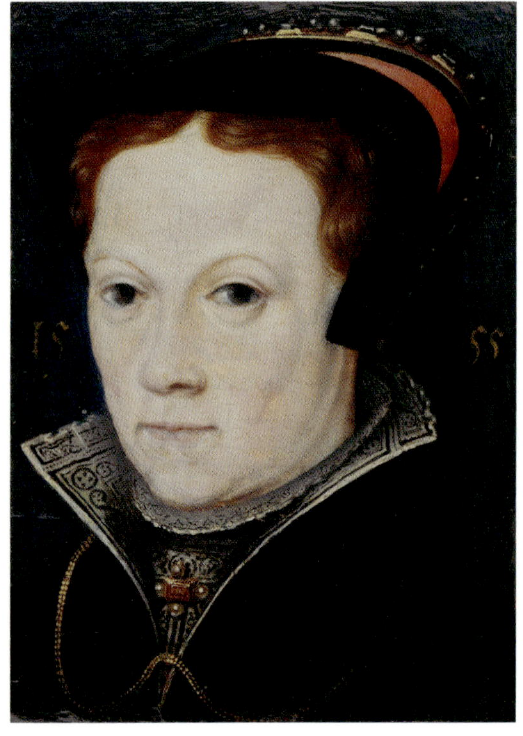

[13]
PHILIP II, KING OF SPAIN
(1527–98)
AFTER TITIAN, 1555

Oil on panel, 86 x 64mm
NPG 4175

[14]
QUEEN MARY I
(1516–58)
AFTER ANTHONIS MOR, 1555

Oil on panel, 86 x 64mm
NPG 4174

The only surviving child of Henry VIII and Katherine of Aragon, Mary (r.1553–58) was declared illegitimate after the annulment of her parents' marriage. She maintained her Roman Catholic faith and, after the death of her half-brother Edward VI, she successfully rallied supporters to claim the throne.

Mary became England's first crowned queen at the age of 37. She married Philip II of Spain the following year and returned England to Catholicism.

When Mary was thought to have become pregnant soon after the marriage, it seemed as if the Roman Catholic succession was secured. However, it proved to be a false pregnancy, and Philip left England, returning only briefly in 1557 in order to gather support for war against France.

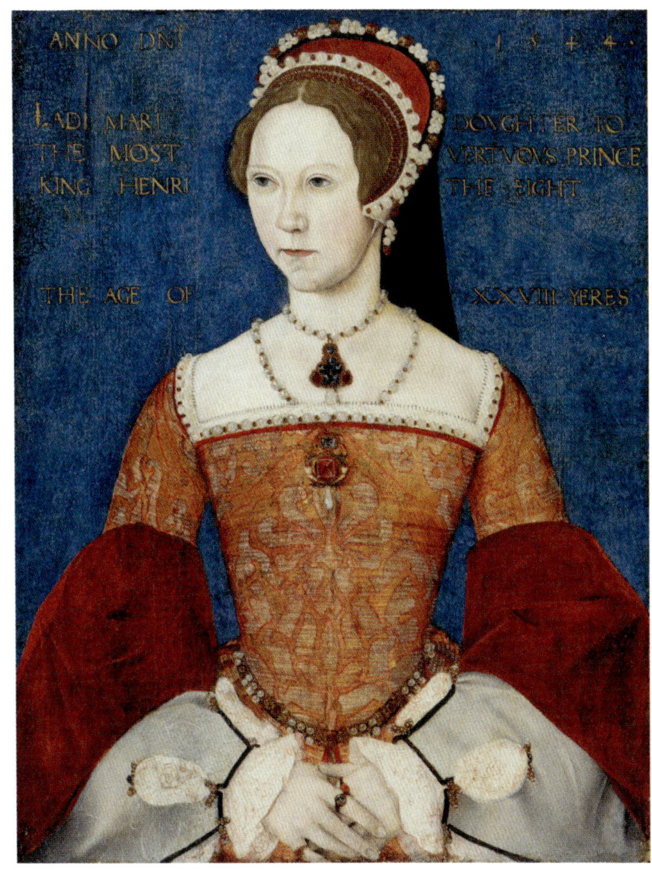

[15]
QUEEN MARY I
ATTRIBUTED TO MASTER JOHN, 1544

Oil on panel, 711 x 508mm
NPG 428

When Elizabeth (r.1558–1603) was born to Henry VIII and Anne Boleyn in 1533, she became heir presumptive to the throne. Following the execution of her mother, Elizabeth was declared illegitimate and was removed from the line of succession. She was restored to her position during the reign of her father's sixth queen, Katherine Parr.

Elizabeth was 25 years old when she inherited the throne from her half-sister Mary in 1558. Elizabeth's reign was characterised by the growth of foreign trade and exploration, and a flourishing literary culture.

Politically shrewd, Elizabeth realised that her position as queen would be undermined if she married. Although she had a number of male favourites and entertained suitors from Sweden, Austria and France, she chose, as she stated in her first address to Parliament: 'to live and die a virgin'.

In this portrait Elizabeth wears a phoenix jewel; the mythical bird was an emblem of rebirth and chastity.

[16]
QUEEN ELIZABETH I
(1533–1603)
NICHOLAS HILLIARD, c.1575

Oil on panel, 787 x 610mm
NPG 190

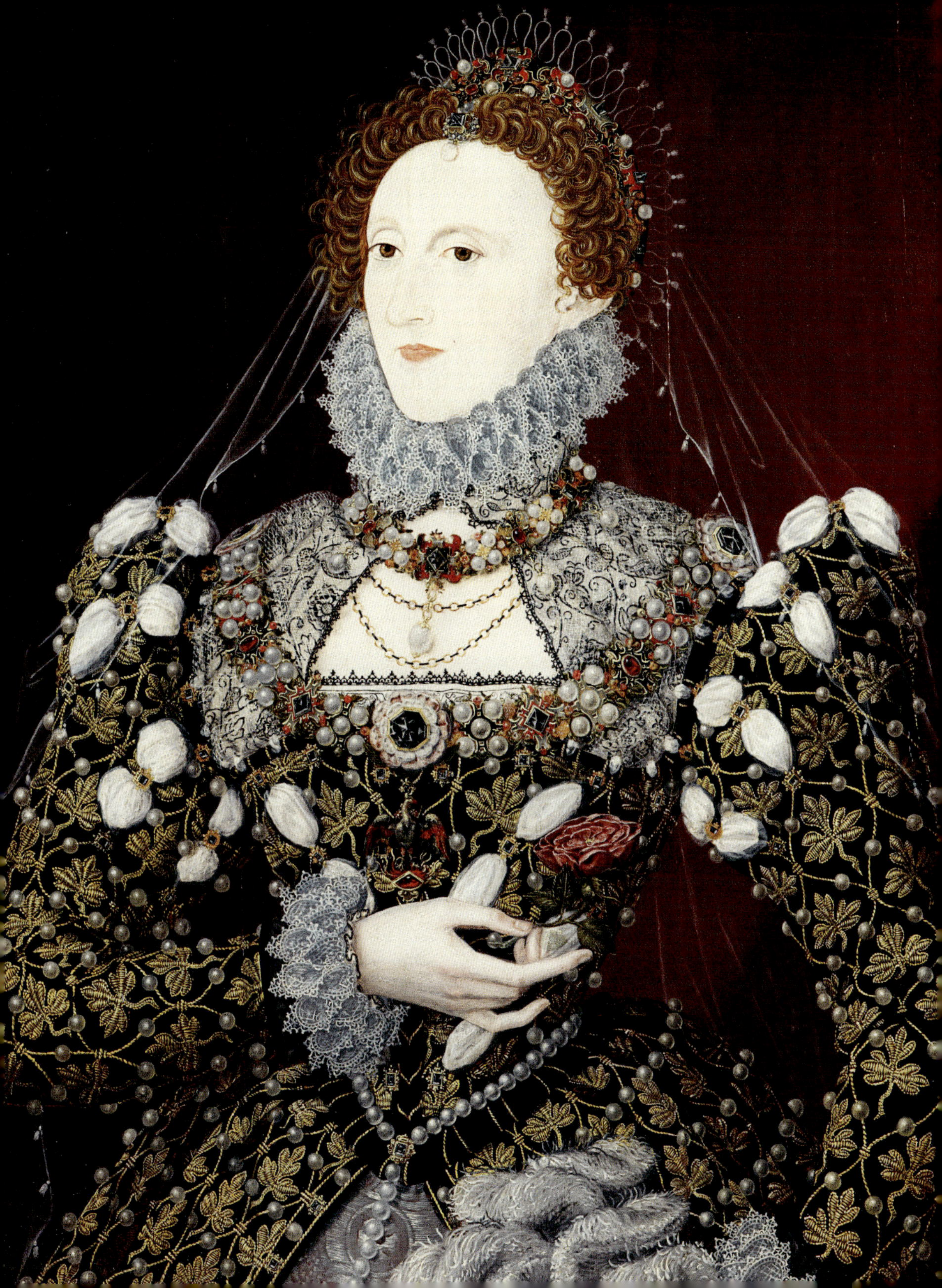

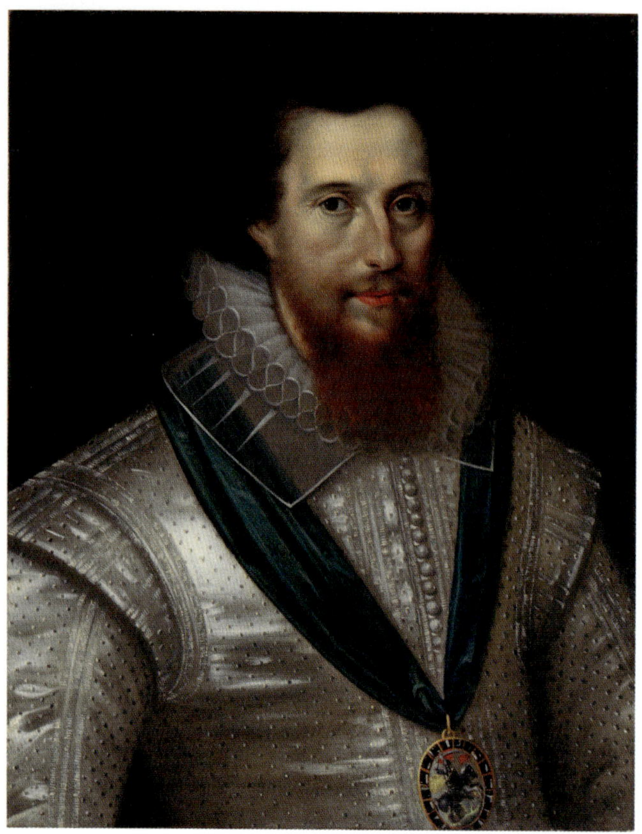

Although Elizabeth I never married, she enjoyed the company of men and had several favourites throughout her reign. The first and greatest of these was Robert Dudley, Earl of Leicester. He was Elizabeth's only serious English suitor, but his status as a subject, combined with the mysterious circumstances of his first wife's death, made him an unsuitable choice for the queen.

Elizabeth's last favourite was the brave but impulsive Robert Devereux, 2nd Earl of Essex. Essex, the stepson of the Earl of Leicester, was always conscious of his public image and regularly sat for his portrait. He became a popular hero following his attack on Cadiz, Spain, in 1596, but grew too confident and overstepped his position by attempting to raise a rebellion against the queen's ministers in 1601. He was arrested, found guilty of treason and executed.

[17]
ROBERT DEVEREUX, 2nd EARL OF ESSEX
(1565–1601)
AFTER MARCUS GHEERAERTS THE YOUNGER, EARLY 17th CENTURY, BASED ON A WORK OF c.1596

Oil on canvas, 635 x 508mm
NPG 180

[18]
ROBERT DUDLEY, EARL OF LEICESTER
(1532/3–88)
UNKNOWN ARTIST, c.1575

Oil on panel, 1080 x 826mm
NPG 447

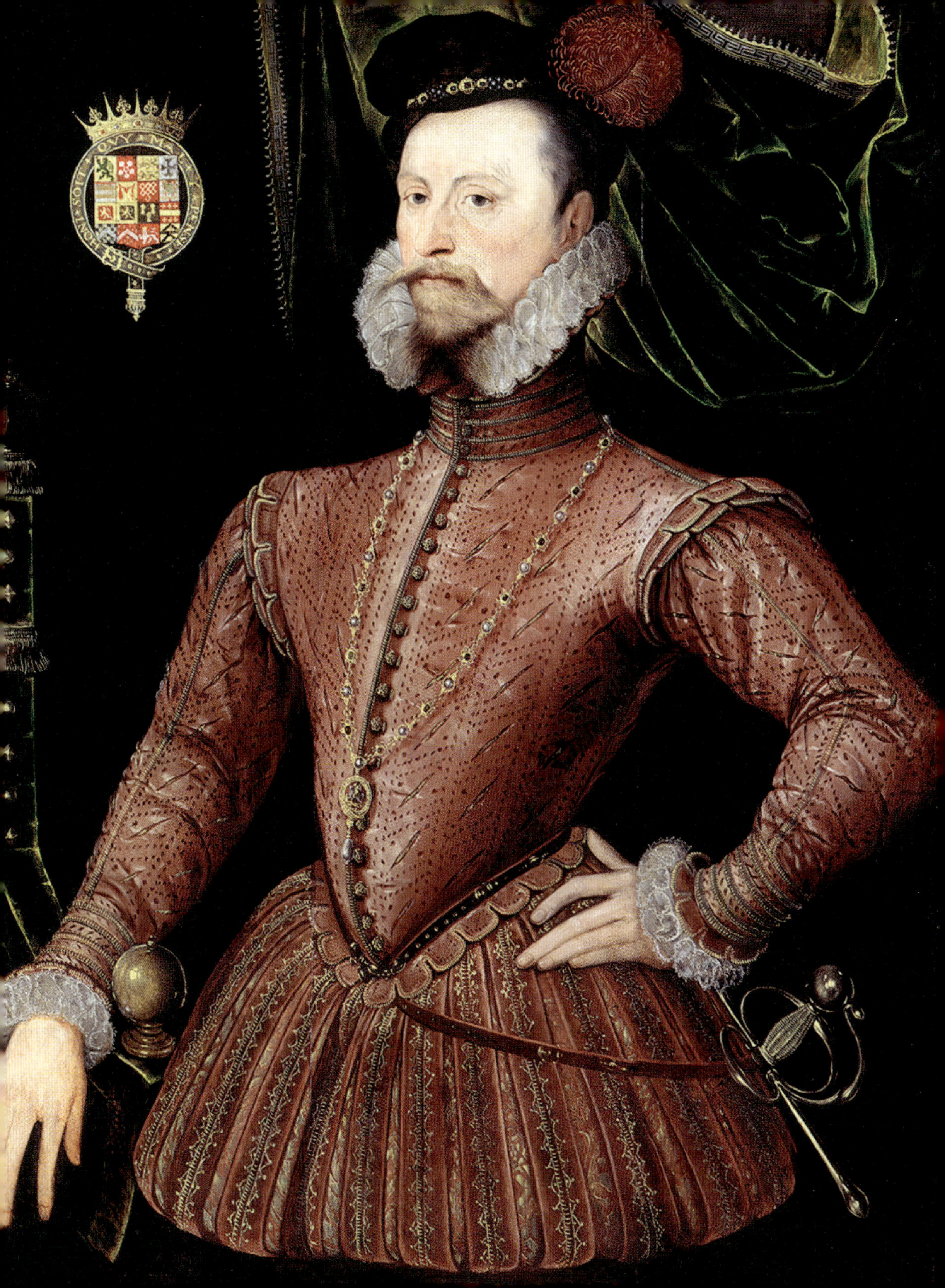

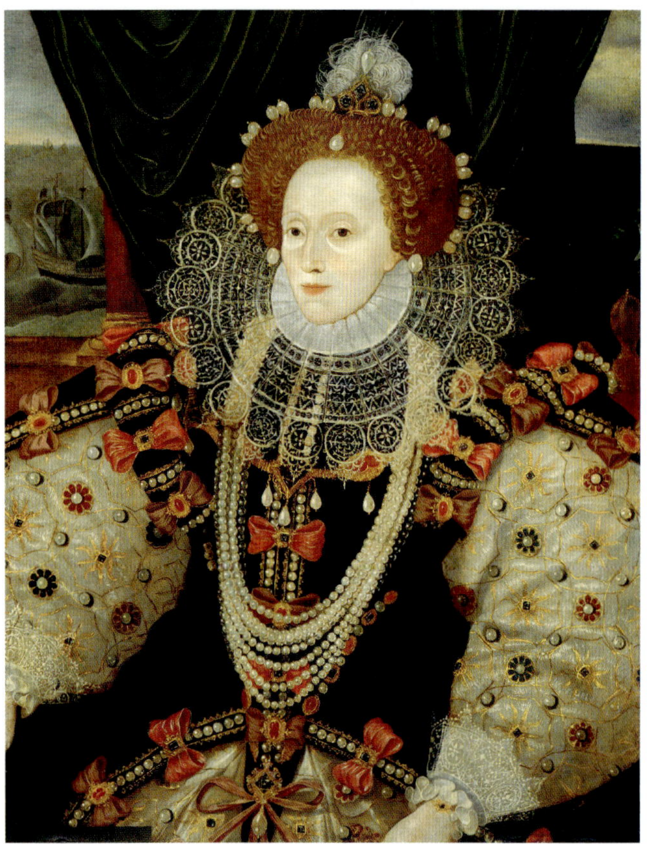

England returned to Protestantism under Elizabeth I. She surrounded herself with able statesmen and advisers, such as William Cecil, 1st Baron Burghley, and together they brought about the re-establishment of the Protestant Church of England through the Acts of Uniformity. However, Elizabeth's long reign was overshadowed by conflict with Spain, and by the threat that foreign powers might try to place Elizabeth's Catholic cousin, Mary, Queen of Scots, on the English throne.

This portrait was produced to commemorate the English defeat of the Spanish Armada in 1588.

[19]
QUEEN ELIZABETH I
(1533–1603)
UNKNOWN ARTIST, c.1588

Oil on panel, 978 x 724mm
NPG 541

Mary became Queen of Scotland as an infant. She married the heir to the French throne, becoming Queen of France in 1559; however, she was widowed aged only 18.

Mary returned to Scotland but was forced to abdicate and flee to England in 1568 after her second husband, Lord Darnley, was murdered and she married Lord Bothwell, the man accused of the murder.

As the great-granddaughter of Henry VII, Mary was key to Catholic attempts to remove the Protestant Queen Elizabeth I. After years of imprisonment in England, she was executed in 1587 when evidence was found of her involvement in a plot to assassinate Elizabeth.

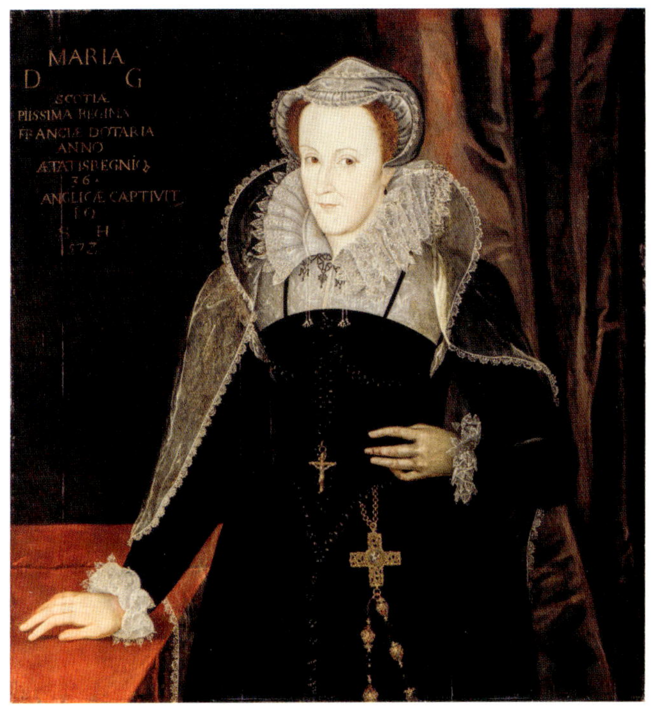

[20]
MARY, QUEEN OF SCOTS
(1542–87)
AFTER NICHOLAS HILLIARD, INSCRIBED 1578

Oil on panel, 791 x 902mm
NPG 429

THE STUARTS

1603–1714

Previous spread (detail)
KING CHARLES I
GERRIT VAN HONTHORST, 1628

Oil on canvas, 762 x 641mm
NPG 4444

On Elizabeth's death in 1603, James VI of Scotland was crowned James I of England. The Stuarts took the place of the Tudors and for the first time England and Scotland were ruled by the same monarch. James's son, Charles I, succeeded him in 1625. Charles's imposition of unpopular taxes, restrictions on the freedom of worship and autocratic rule led to civil war between Parliamentarians and Royalists. Charles was tried and executed by Parliament in 1649, the only British monarch to be executed by his subjects.

After the death of the king, the leader of the Parliamentarians, Oliver Cromwell, established a republic that lasted until 1660. He was made Lord Protector in 1653. The role passed briefly to his son, but without support, Richard Cromwell's Protectorate failed.

In 1660, Charles I's eldest son was invited by Parliament to return from exile abroad to reign as Charles II. His return was met with public rejoicing and optimism, but this was soon replaced by concern about his tolerance of Catholicism and friendship with France, as well as a series of disasters including plague, fire and war.

When Charles II died, the throne passed to his Catholic brother James II. The birth of a son brought anxieties about a Catholic succession to a head. A group of politicians invited the Protestant William of Orange, husband of James II's daughter Mary, to invade England. William's invasion met little resistance, and James and his family fled the country.

William III and Mary II reigned together until Mary's death in 1694, after which William reigned alone until 1702. He was succeeded on the throne by Mary's younger sister Anne. Her death in 1714, without an heir, ended over a century of Stuart rule.

At the age of one, James was crowned King of Scotland following the abdication of his mother, Mary, Queen of Scots. He married Anne of Denmark in 1590 and they went on to have seven children – only three of whom survived beyond infancy.

In 1603, when James (r.1603–25) inherited the throne of England from his cousin Elizabeth I, Scotland shared a monarch for the first time with England, Wales and Ireland.

Committed to peace, James attempted to balance religious divisions and successfully held the four nations together. However, his handling of finances was disastrous, creating a difficult legacy for his son, Charles.

This late representation, showing him in the robes of the Order of the Garter, celebrates the role he cast himself in as a peacemaker in Europe, with the inscription *Beati pacifici* (Blessed are the peacemakers) above him.

[21]
KING JAMES I OF ENGLAND AND VI OF SCOTLAND
(1566–1625)
DANIEL MYTENS, 1621

Oil on canvas, 1486 x 1006mm
NPG 109

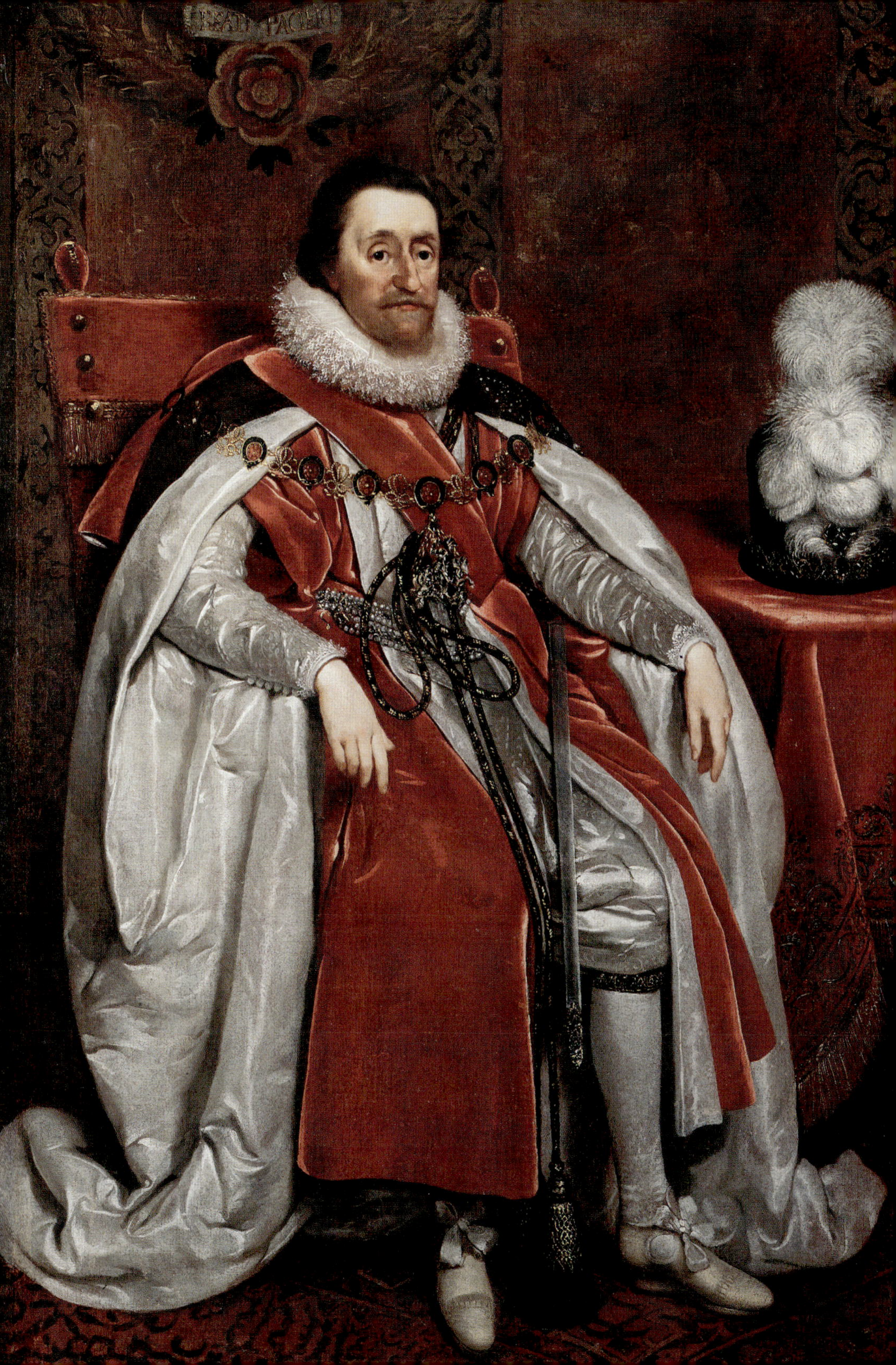

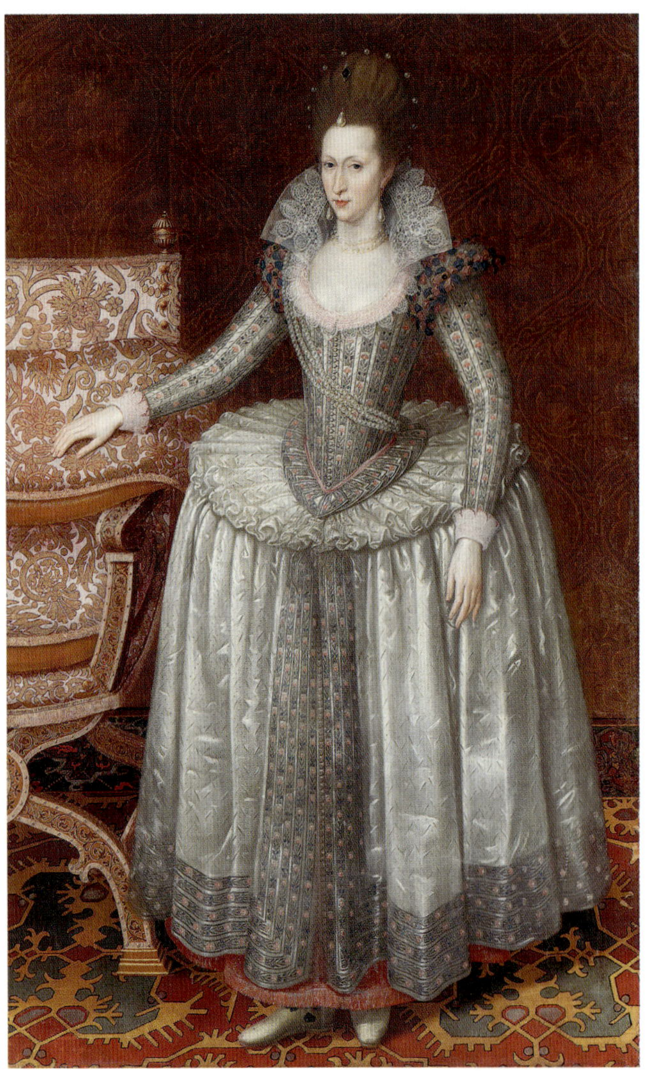

Anne was a daughter of the king and queen of Denmark, Frederick II and Sophie of Mecklenburg-Güstrow. She married James VI of Scotland shortly before she turned 15, in 1589. She had seven children with James, of whom three – Henry, Elizabeth and Charles – lived beyond childhood.

After James's accession to the English throne in 1603, Anne became one of the most important patrons of her day. She commissioned artists, architects, composers, choreographers and writers. Ben Jonson created elaborate court masques for her. These extraordinary, lavish theatrical performances celebrated the role of the monarchy. Anne promoted prestigious international marriages for her children and a European court culture in England.

[22]
ANNE OF DENMARK
(1574–1619)
JOHN DE CRITZ THE ELDER, c.1606–8

Oil on canvas, 2016 x 1265mm
NPG 6918

Handsome and ambitious, George Villiers, 1st Duke of Buckingham, was the most influential of a number of close male friends or favourites of James I. This portrait celebrates Buckingham's power and his much-admired looks. He wears the robes and insignia of the Order of the Garter; Knights of the Garter were, at this time, a select group of the most powerful men in the kingdom.

Buckingham became one of the king's leading ministers and was an effective administrator. However, he was widely regarded as corrupt and extravagant and was blamed for military failures in Spain and France. In 1628, Buckingham was murdered by a disgruntled soldier.

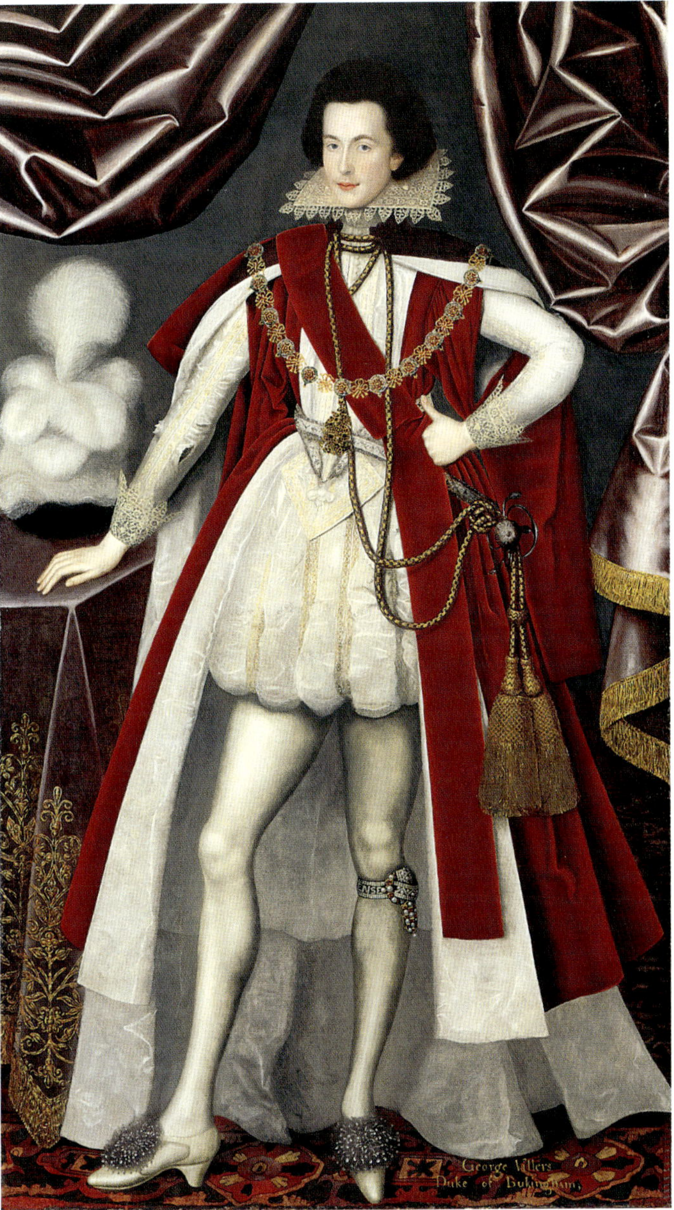

[23]
GEORGE VILLIERS, 1st DUKE OF BUCKINGHAM
(1592–1628)
STUDIO OF WILLIAM LARKIN, c.1616

Oil on canvas, 2057 x 1194mm
NPG 3840

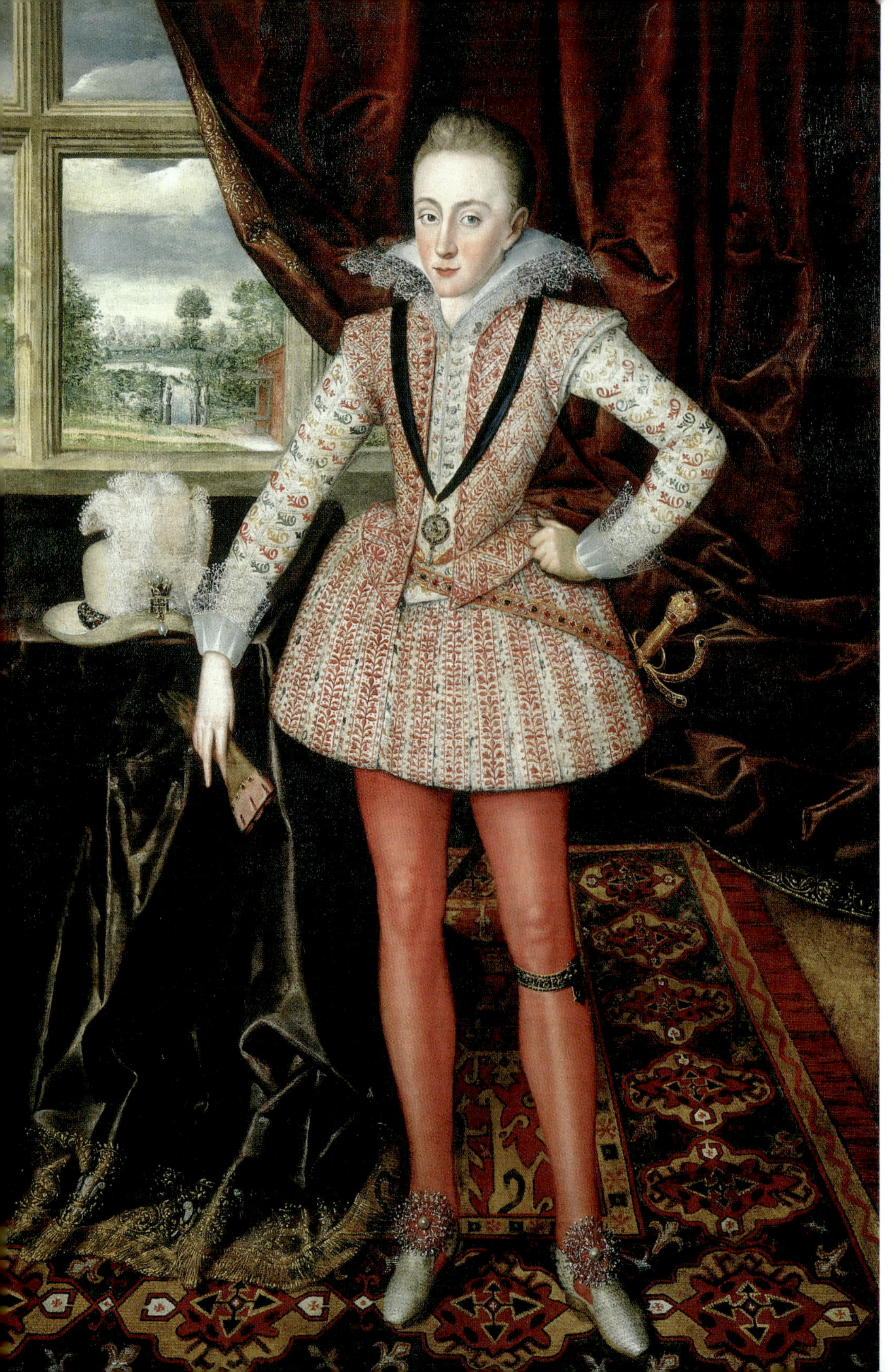

James I and Anne of Denmark had three surviving children: Henry, Elizabeth and Charles. Henry, Prince of Wales, was seen as a particularly promising prince. He died tragically in 1612, aged only 18. His death was a blow to the hopes of many in England who supported the clever and cultured prince, and prompted widespread mourning. The throne was instead inherited by their second son, who became Charles I.

Elizabeth was also a focus for hope and expectation, and an important pawn in the game of international royal marriage negotiations. She was married at the age of 16 to Frederick V, Elector Palatine. In 1619, Frederick accepted the throne of Bohemia, where they reigned for less than a year before being ousted by the armies of the Roman Catholic Habsburg emperor, Ferdinand II. The rest of Elizabeth's life, much of it as a widow, was lived in exile in The Hague.

[24]
HENRY, PRINCE OF WALES
(1594–1612)
ROBERT PEAKE THE ELDER, c.1610

Oil on canvas, 1727 x 1137mm
NPG 4515

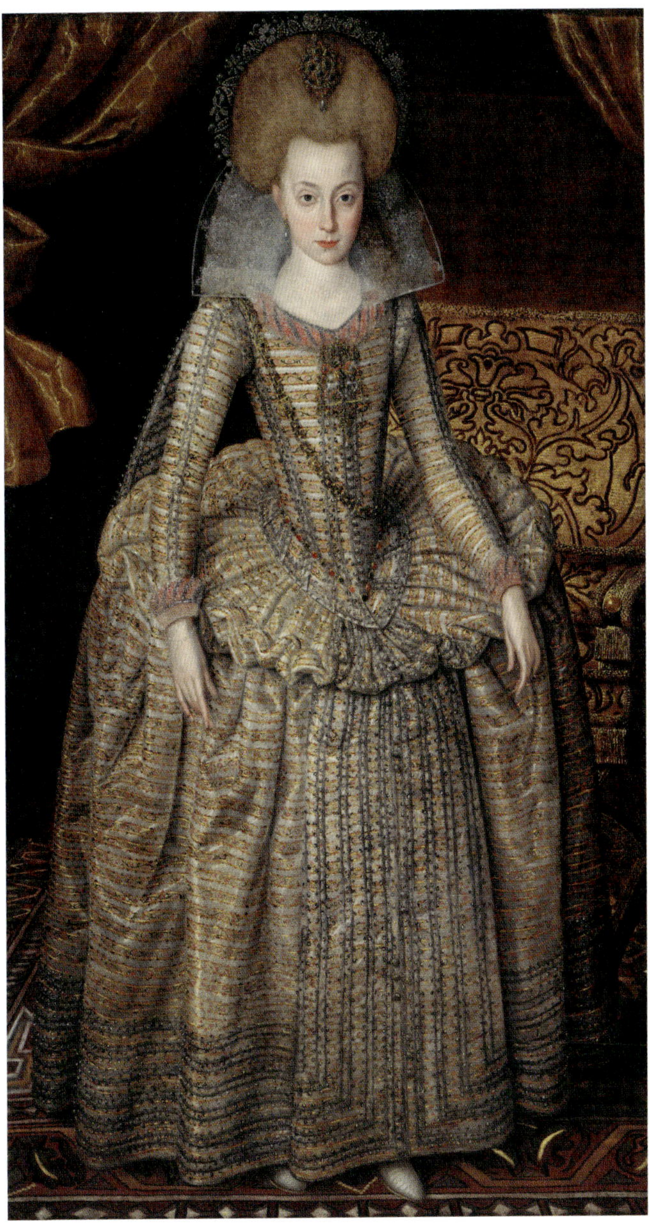

[25]
PRINCESS ELIZABETH, QUEEN OF BOHEMIA AND ELECTRESS PALATINE
(1596–1641)
ROBERT PEAKE THE ELDER, c.1610

Oil on canvas, 1713 x 968mm
NPG 6113

The younger son of James I and Anne of Denmark, Charles (r.1625–49) became heir to the throne on the death of his older brother, Henry in 1612. He had a speech impediment and experienced physical disabilities when young, which led to comparisons with his much-admired elder brother. His personal life flourished, however, with a successful marriage to Henrietta Maria of France. They had six children who survived beyond early childhood.

Charles's dismissal of Parliament and imposition of unpopular taxes, along with his attempts to impose religious uniformity, contributed to increasing civil and political unrest. This eventually culminated in war between the three kingdoms of England, Scotland and Ireland, civil wars in England, and Charles's execution in 1649.

[26]
KING CHARLES I
(1600–49)
DANIEL MYTENS, 1631

Oil on canvas, 2159 x 1346mm
NPG 1246

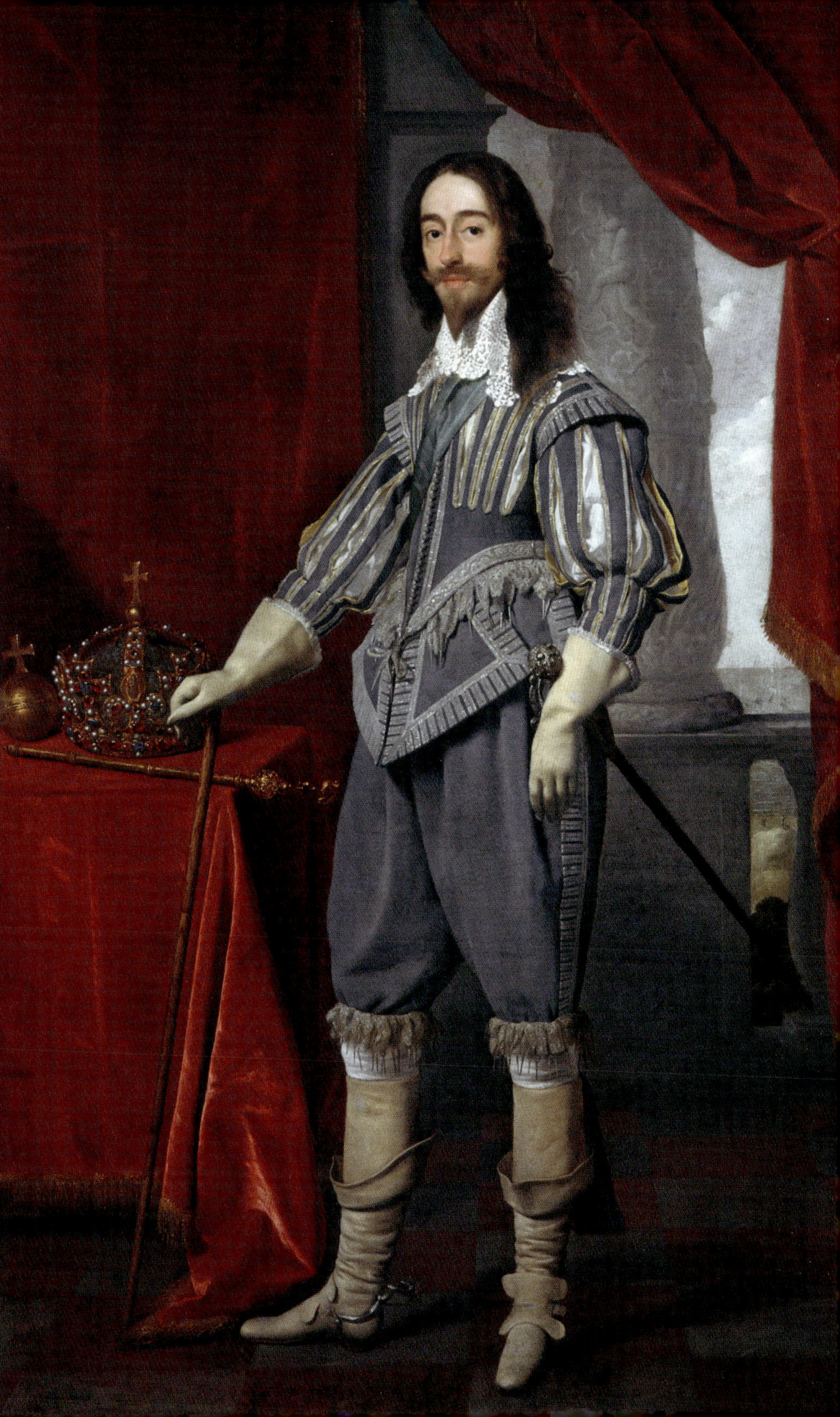

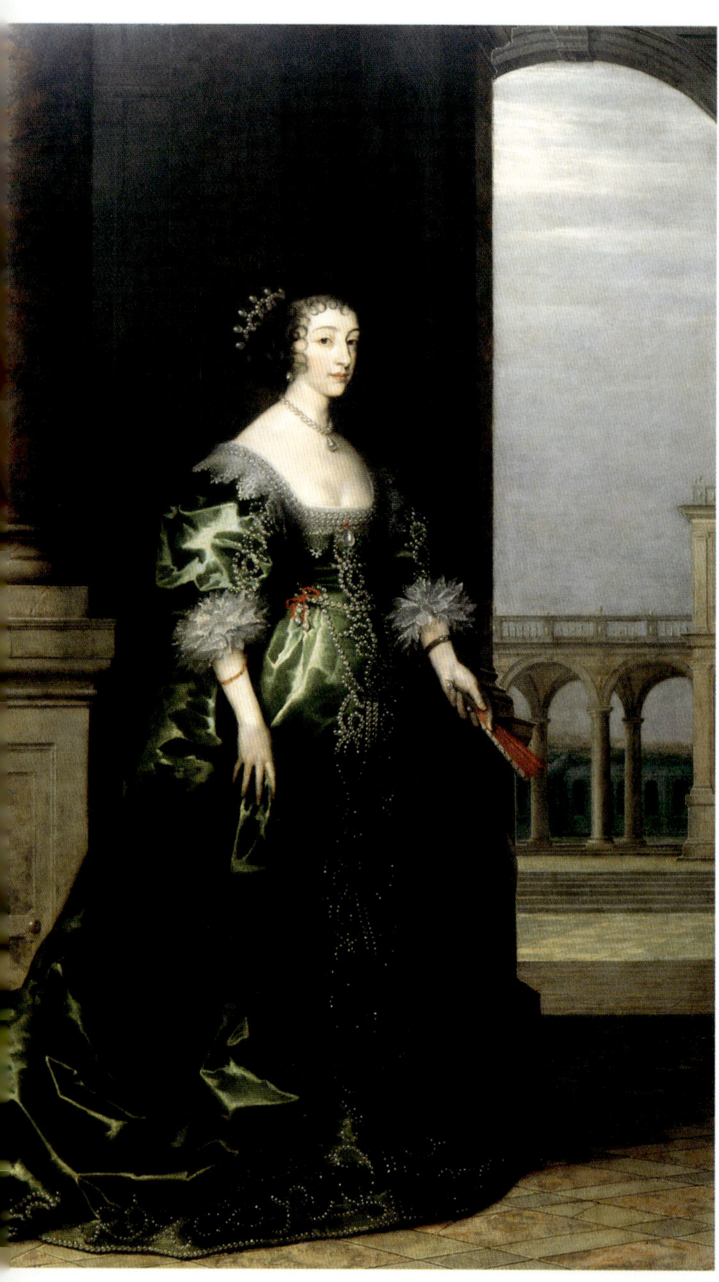

Henrietta Maria was a daughter of Henri IV of France and Marie de' Medici. Her marriage to Charles I in 1625 was a result of James I's policy to establish allies in Europe through the marriages of his children. After a rocky start, Henrietta's relationship with Charles flourished. She gave birth to nine children and their family life was happy, as reflected in the works of the court painter Sir Anthony van Dyck.

When Charles's coronation took place, Henrietta refused to be crowned by a Protestant bishop. Her Catholicism was to be a source of tension throughout Charles's reign.

During the civil wars, Henrietta returned to France, where she pawned her jewellery to raise funds and worked hard to get diplomatic and practical help for the Royalists. She returned to England in the early 1660s after the monarchy was restored but eventually settled back in France, where she died.

[27]
HENRIETTA MARIA
(1609–69)
UNKNOWN ARTIST, BACKGROUND BY HENDRIK VAN STEENWYCK, c.1635

Oil on canvas, 2159 x 1352mm
NPG 1247

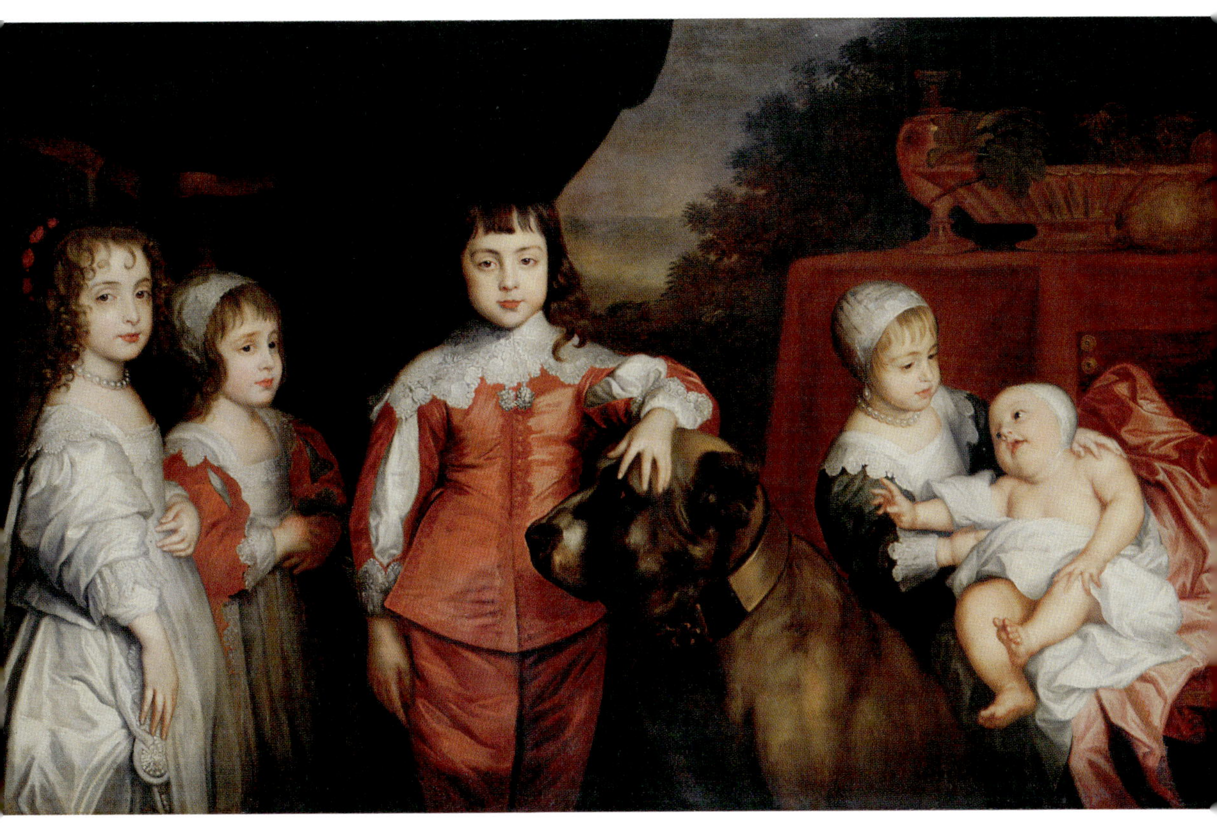

[28]
FIVE CHILDREN OF KING CHARLES I
PRINCESS MARY (1631–60); PRINCE JAMES (1633–1701); PRINCE CHARLES (1630–85); PRINCESS ELIZABETH (1635–50); PRINCESS ANNE (1637–40)

AFTER SIR ANTHONY VAN DYCK, 17th CENTURY, BASED ON A WORK OF 1637
Oil on canvas, 895 x 1762mm
NPG 267

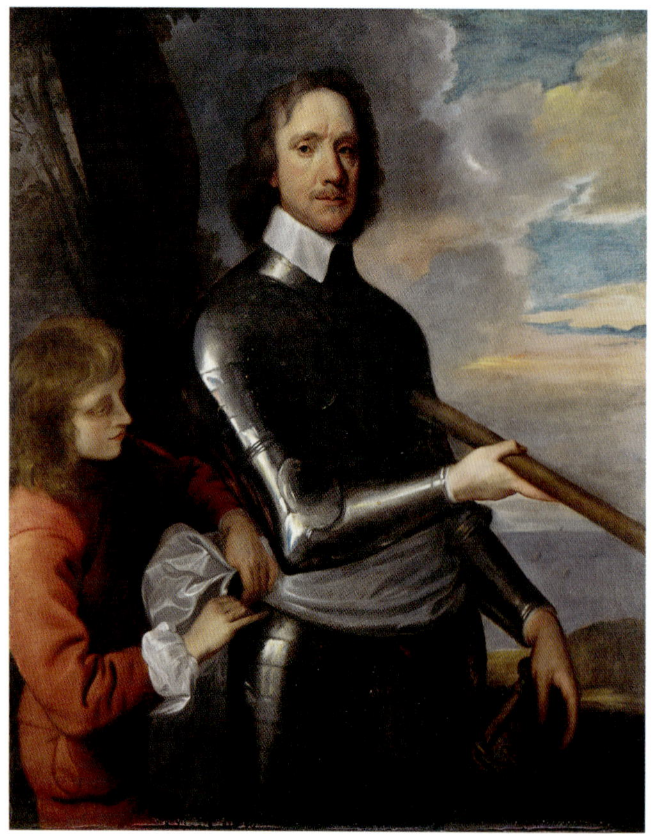

Oliver Cromwell rose from the position of a country gentleman to become a leading statesman, soldier and finally head of state as Lord Protector (1653–58).

As a Puritan, Cromwell was distrustful of Charles I and felt that the Church of England was insufficiently Protestant. As the country descended into civil war, he emerged as a natural leader. Along with his Parliamentarian supporters, he defeated Charles I and authorised the king's eventual execution in 1649. Cromwell's son, Richard, briefly took over following his father's death in 1658, but he lacked the same authority and resigned after nine months.

This painting is based on Anthony van Dyck's portraits of Charles I's court. The visual references to Cromwell's military command – his armour, baton and the sash being tied by an attendant – are all borrowed from paintings produced for the regime he had just overthrown.

[29]
OLIVER CROMWELL
(1599–1658)
ROBERT WALKER, c.1649

Oil on canvas, 1257 x 1016mm
NPG 536

Charles was the eldest child of Charles I. He spent most of his youth in exile on the continent during the Republic. In 1660, he was invited by Parliament to return from abroad to become King Charles II (r.1660–85).

The return of the king was met with celebration and hope. Puritan restraint was lifted: the theatres reopened and women appeared for the first time on the stage. Charles II's court, however, was soon criticised for excess and debauchery, and his reign was beset with conspiracies and plots, as well as major disasters, such as the Plague, the Great Fire of London and the Dutch attack of the Medway.

He had 14 children with his many mistresses, but none with his Portuguese queen, Catherine of Braganza. Perceived as cynical, lazy and notorious for saying one thing and doing another, Charles was also charming and approachable, and promoted science and technology with genuine interest.

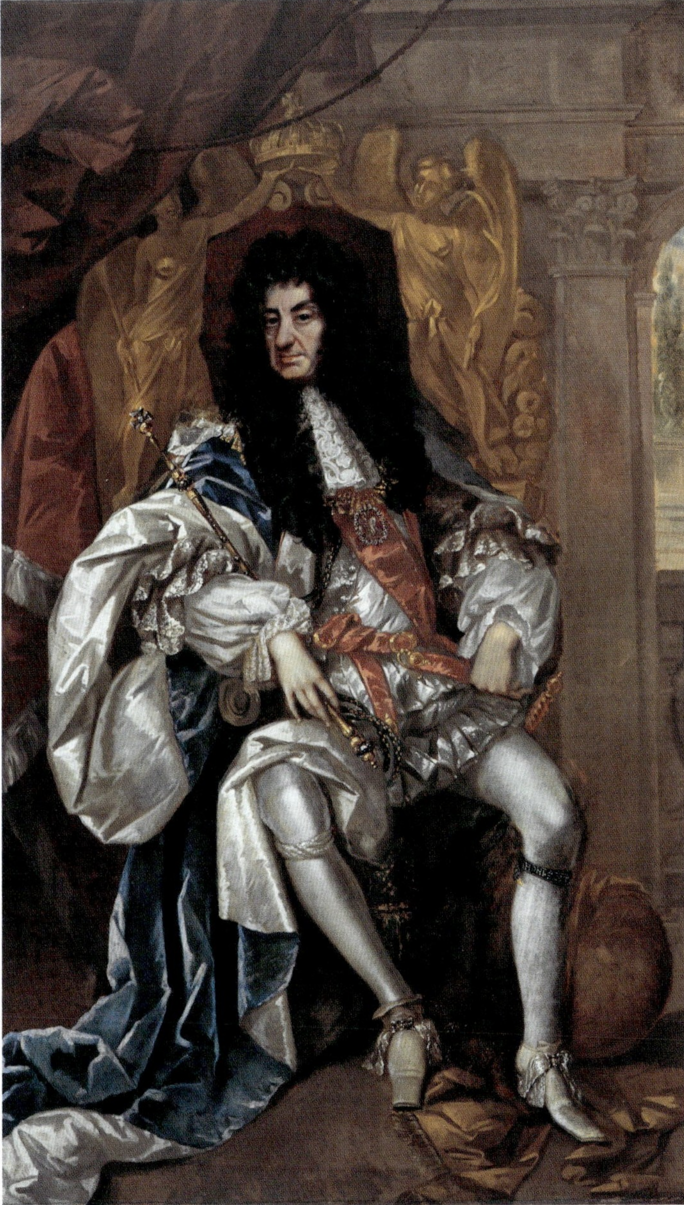

[30]
KING CHARLES II
(1630–85)
ATTRIBUTED TO THOMAS HAWKER, c.1680

Oil on canvas, 2267 x 1356mm
NPG 4691

Catherine of Braganza was a daughter of the king and queen of Portugal, John IV and Luisa de Guzmán. She married Charles II in 1662. A huge dowry was agreed, which included control of Tangier in Morocco and Bombay in India and about £300,000. There was also a free trade agreement with Brazil and the East Indies, which aided Britain's global expansion.

Catherine is shown wearing Portuguese court dress. Her fashions were mocked when she came to England and she quickly abandoned them, adopting English court style.

Charles and Catherine had no children, although Charles had many children with his mistresses. After Charles's death and the succession of his brother, James II, to the throne, Catherine lived quietly in retirement until she returned to Portugal in 1692.

[31]
CATHERINE OF BRAGANZA
(1638–1705)
BY OR AFTER DIRCK STOOP, c.1660–1

Oil on canvas, 1232 x 1003mm
NPG 2563

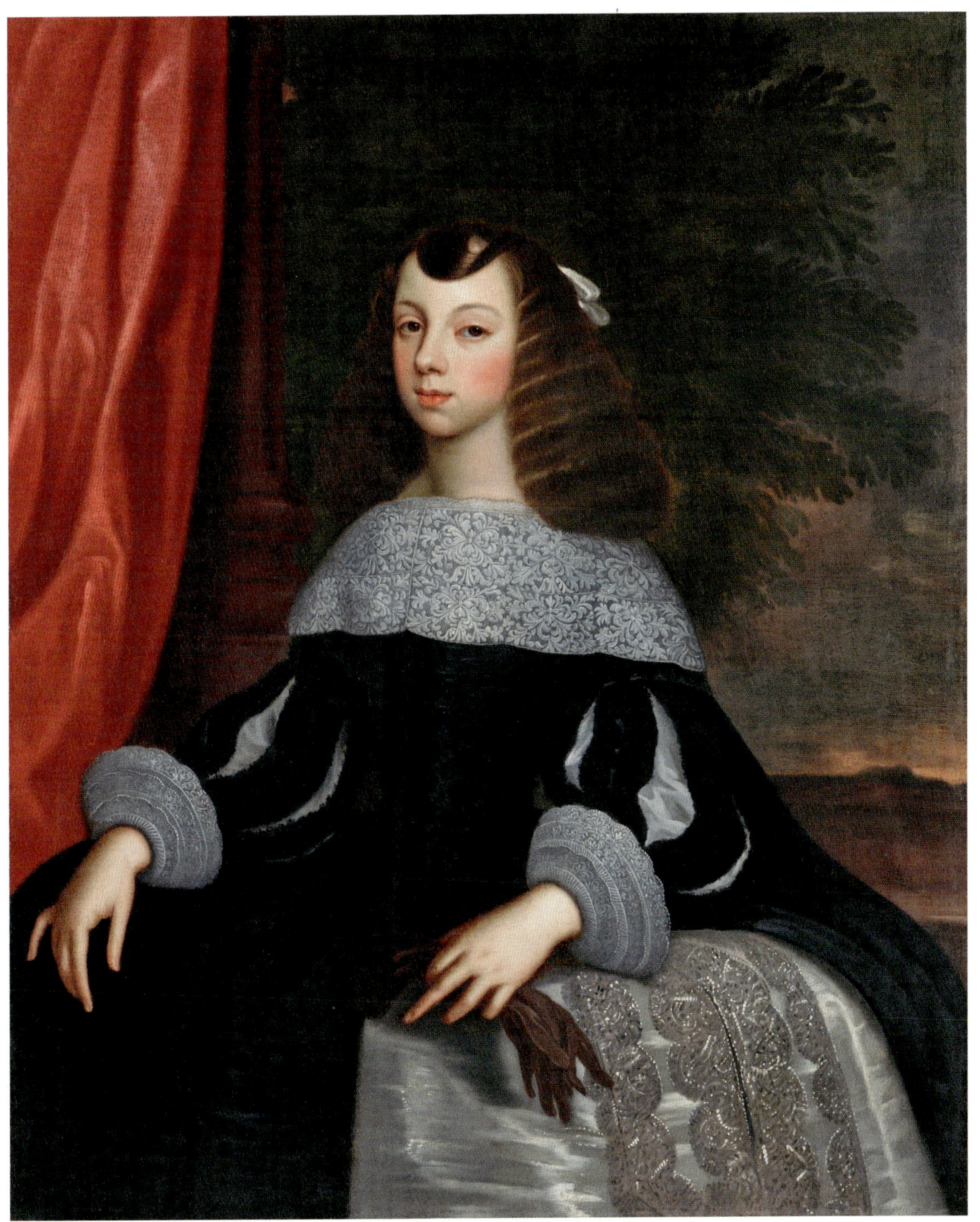

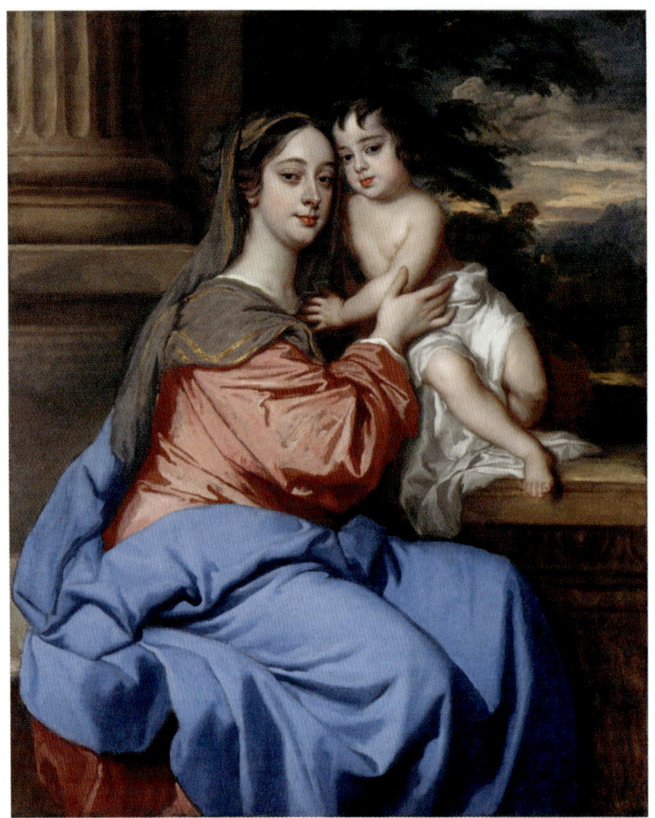

Barbara Villiers was Charles II's mistress when he was restored to the throne in 1660. She had at least five children with him, wielded political influence by facilitating access to him and was more prominent at court than his wife, Catherine of Braganza.

Famous for her beauty, she was despised by many for her indulgent lifestyle, symbolising the excess and promiscuity of the Restoration court.

Portraits of Barbara were greatly in demand, this work was created by Peter Lely, the king's Principal Painter. It shows Barbara as the Virgin Mary with her eldest son by the king as the Christ Child.

[32]
BARBARA VILLIERS, DUCHESS OF CLEVELAND, WITH HER SON, CHARLES FITZROY
(1640–1709; 1662–1730)
SIR PETER LELY, c.1664

Oil on canvas, 1247 x 1020mm
NPG 6725

Nell Gwyn began her career as an orange-seller to theatregoers. She rose to become one of the most famous comic actors of her day, and one of the first women to perform in public.

In the late 1660s, she became a mistress of Charles II. They had two sons and the elder was created Duke of St Albans. Charles is said to have remembered her on his deathbed with the words, 'Let not poor Nelly starve'.

The artist Simon Verelst painted Nell a number of times, often in revealing dress, as here. This reflects the fact that female actors were regarded as operating outside the conventions of normal society.

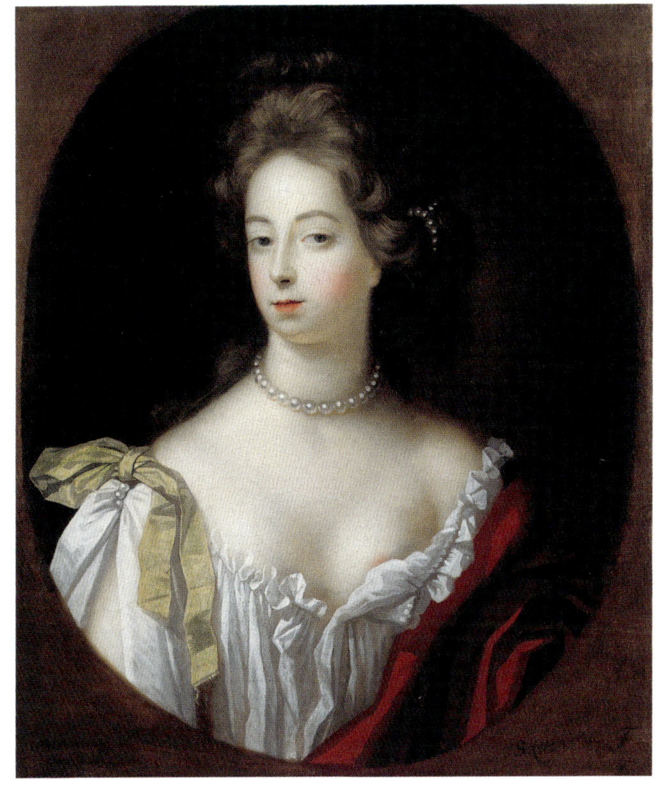

[33]
NELL GWYN
(1644–c.1710)
SIMON VERELST, c.1680

Oil on canvas, 737 x 632mm
NPG 2496

James was the second surviving son of Charles I and Henrietta Maria. During the civil wars, while his father was held prisoner by the Parliamentarians, James was able to escape to the Netherlands. He was married twice: first to Anne Hyde and second to Mary of Modena.

Following the death of his brother, Charles II, James acceded the throne as King James II (r.1685–88), with Mary as queen consort. The first openly Roman Catholic monarch since Mary I, James successfully crushed a rebellion led by Charles's eldest illegitimate son, the Protestant Duke of Monmouth.

James became increasingly unpopular for his religious beliefs, his suspension of Parliament when it disagreed with him and his placing of Catholics in powerful positions. Fearing a Catholic monarchy in perpetuity, a group of powerful politicians invited James's Protestant son-in-law, William of Orange, to invade. James fled into exile after only three years on the throne.

[34]
KING JAMES II
(1633–1701)
SIR GODFREY KNELLER, 1684

Oil on canvas, 2456 x 144mm
NPG 666

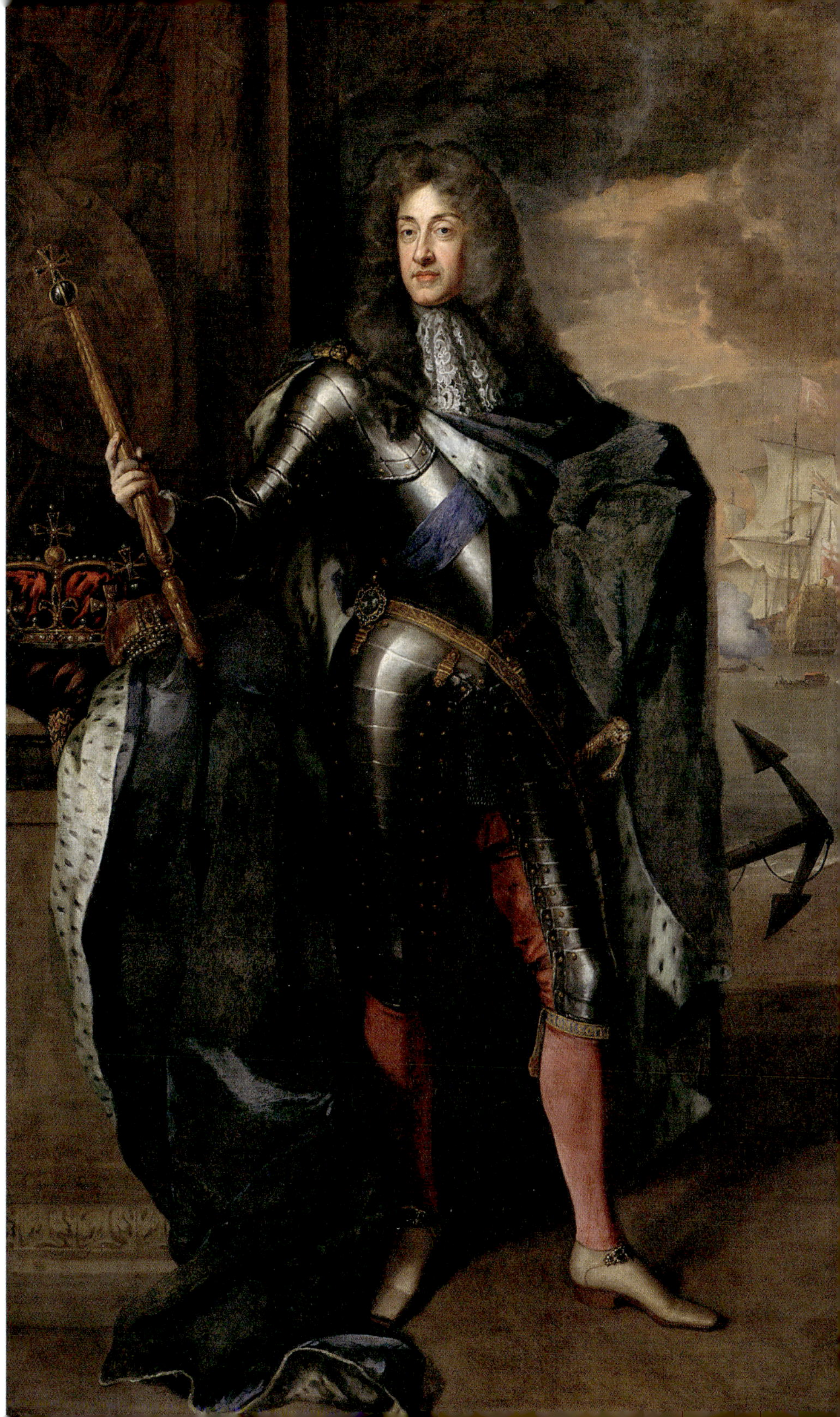

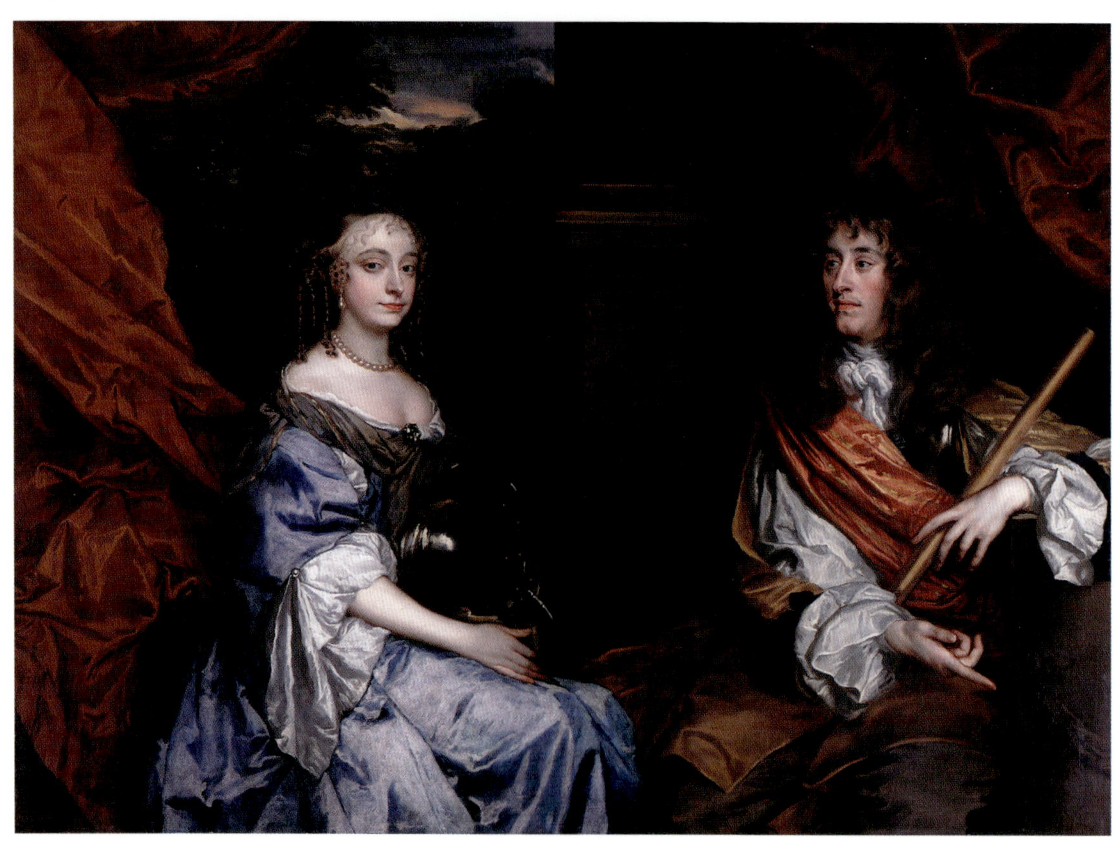

[35]
ANNE HYDE, DUCHESS OF YORK AND KING JAMES II
(1637–71; 1633–1701)
SIR PETER LELY, c.1661–62

Oil on canvas, 1397 x 1920mm
NPG 5077

Anne Hyde was the daughter of Edward Hyde, Earl of Clarendon, who was Charles II's chief minister. Anne and James II had begun a relationship while the court was still in exile on the Continent; Anne became pregnant and, after some uncertainty, James married her. Anne was to die young, shortly after the birth of her last child.

James later married an Italian Catholic princess, Mary of Modena. James inherited the throne from his brother in 1685 and Mary became queen consort. The birth of their son James in 1688 prompted leading politicians to invite William of Orange to invade England, in order to secure a Protestant monarchy.

James and Anne's Protestant daughters, Mary and Anne, would both ascend the throne.

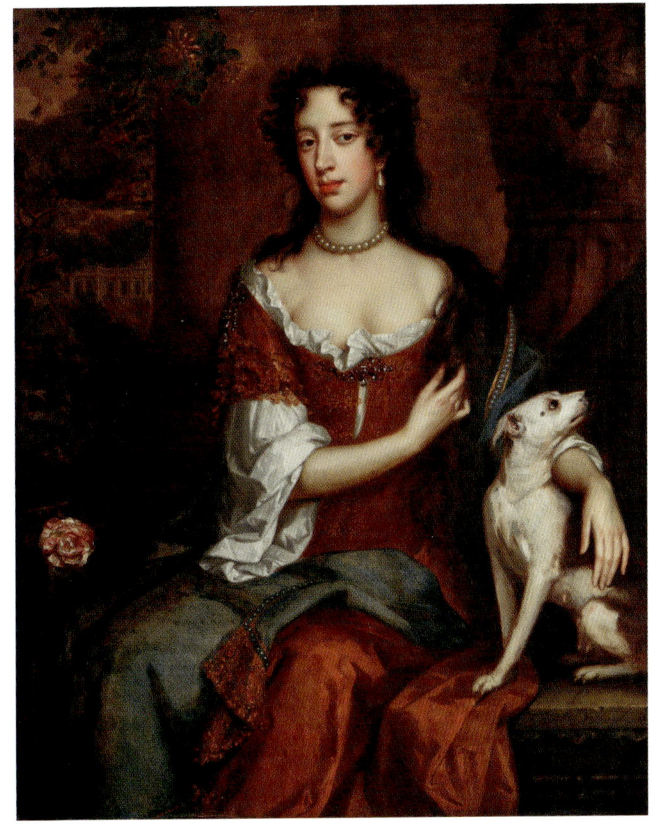

[36]
MARY OF MODENA
(1658–1718)
WILLEM WISSING, c.1685

Oil on canvas, 1220 x 978mm
NPG 214

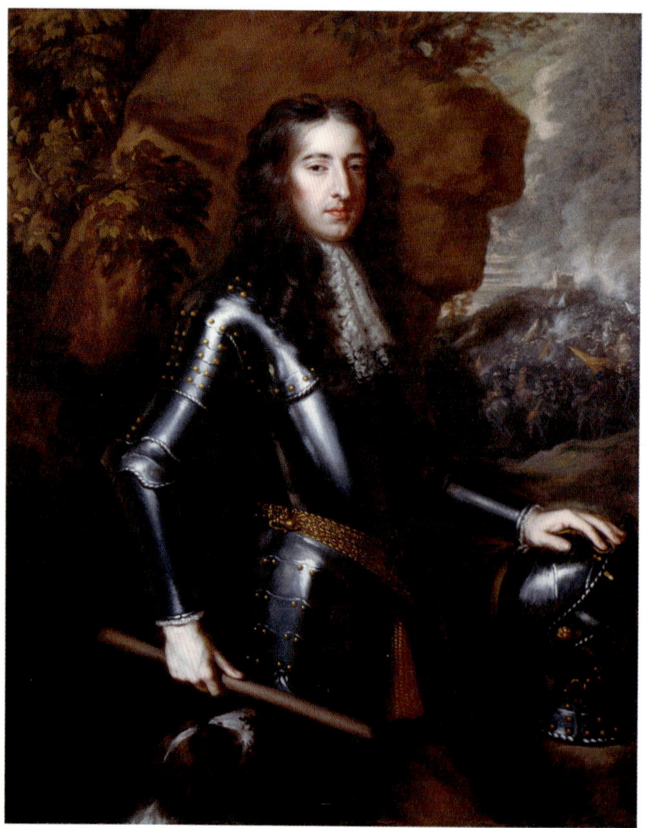

William of Orange (r.1689–1702) was born and raised in the Netherlands and married James II's daughter, Mary, in 1677. William's lifelong ambition was to stop France expanding its territories, and his interactions with Britain were all driven by this goal.

The birth of a son to James II's second wife, the Roman Catholic Mary of Modena, created religious anxieties: the successor to the throne was now likely to be Catholic rather than passing to his Protestant daughter Mary. In response to this, a group of politicians invited William to invade England.

William's invasion met little resistance, and James and his family fled the country. William and Mary were made joint monarchs of England, Scotland and, after much bloodshed, Ireland. Their reign was notable for new restrictions on royal power and increased religious tolerance, but also for war in Europe, battles in Scotland and devastating wars in Ireland.

[37]
KING WILLIAM III
(1650–1702)
STUDIO OF SIR PETER LELY,
BASED ON A WORK OF c.1677

Oil on canvas, 1245 x 1010mm
NPG 1902

The eldest daughter of James II and his first wife Anne Hyde, Mary (r.1689–94) was married to William of Orange at the age of 15. At first, he was indifferent towards her, but their relationship improved and, as a devout Protestant, she supported William's invasion of England in 1688.

Mary was popular both in the Netherlands and in Britain. A wise and effective ruler during William's absences at war, she also led many charitable schemes. William III and Mary II reigned together until Mary's death in 1694, after which William reigned alone until 1702.

Both of these portraits were painted at the time of their marriage. Anne is shown wearing orange, symbolic of the Dutch royal house of which she had just become a member.

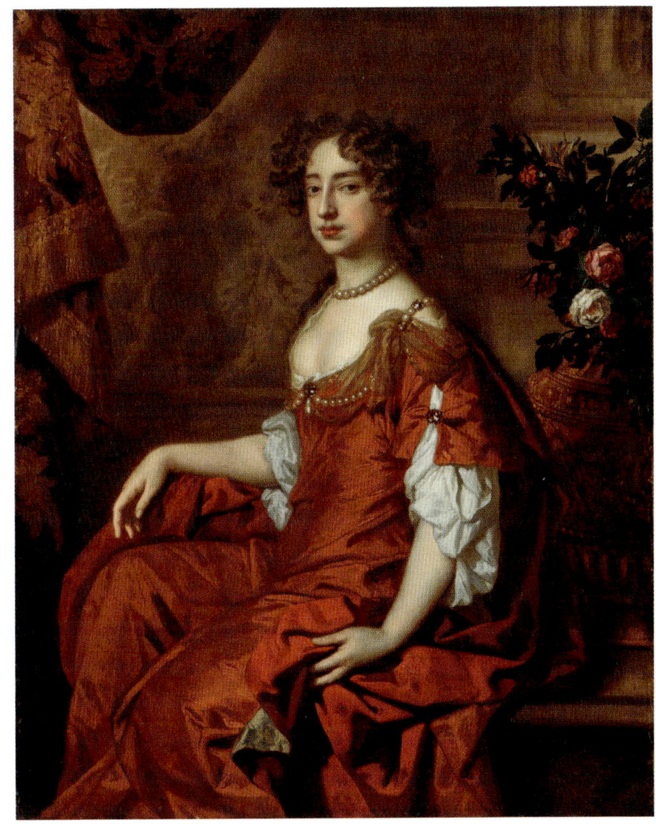

[38]
QUEEN MARY II
(1662–94)
SIR PETER LELY, c.1677

Oil on canvas, 1245 x 1019mm
NPG 6214

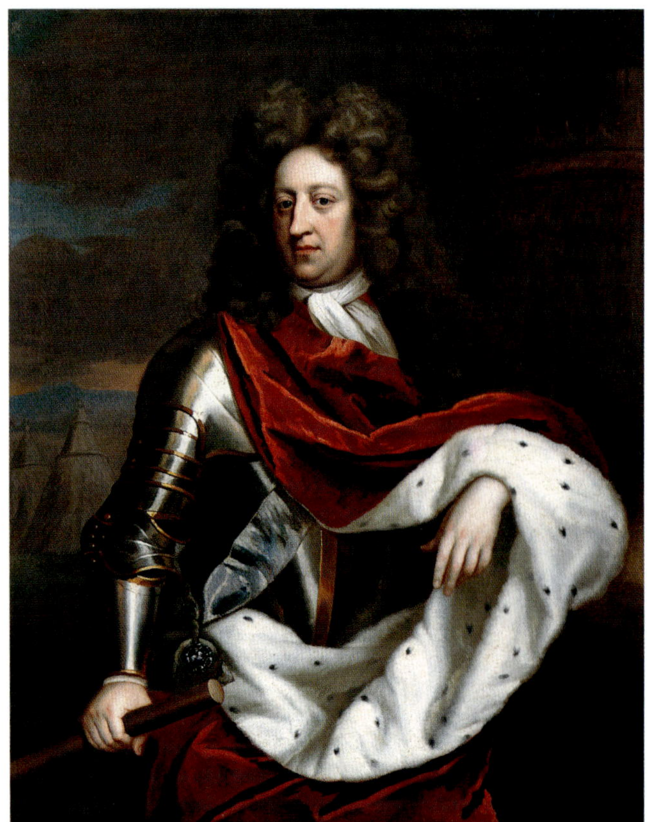

William and Mary were childless so they were succeeded to the throne by Mary's younger sister, Queen Anne (r.1702–14). With her husband, Prince George of Denmark, Anne had at least 17 pregnancies in 17 years, but only five live births, and just one child who lived beyond infancy, only to die at the age of eleven.

During Anne's reign, Britain achieved major military victories against France and Spain, and diplomatic success. Her achievements included the Act of Union between England and Scotland in 1707, bringing the two countries together as a single kingdom. Her personal power was diminished by the development of Britain's constitutional monarchy, which increasingly gave Parliament authority over the crown. Her death in 1714 without an heir ended over a century of Stuart rule.

[39]
PRINCE GEORGE OF DENMARK
(1653–1708)
AFTER MICHAEL DAHL, c.1705

Oil on canvas, 1257 x 1029mm
NPG 4163

[40]
QUEEN ANNE
(1665–1714)
MICHAEL DAHL, c.1702

Oil on canvas, 2368 x 1448mm
NPG 6187

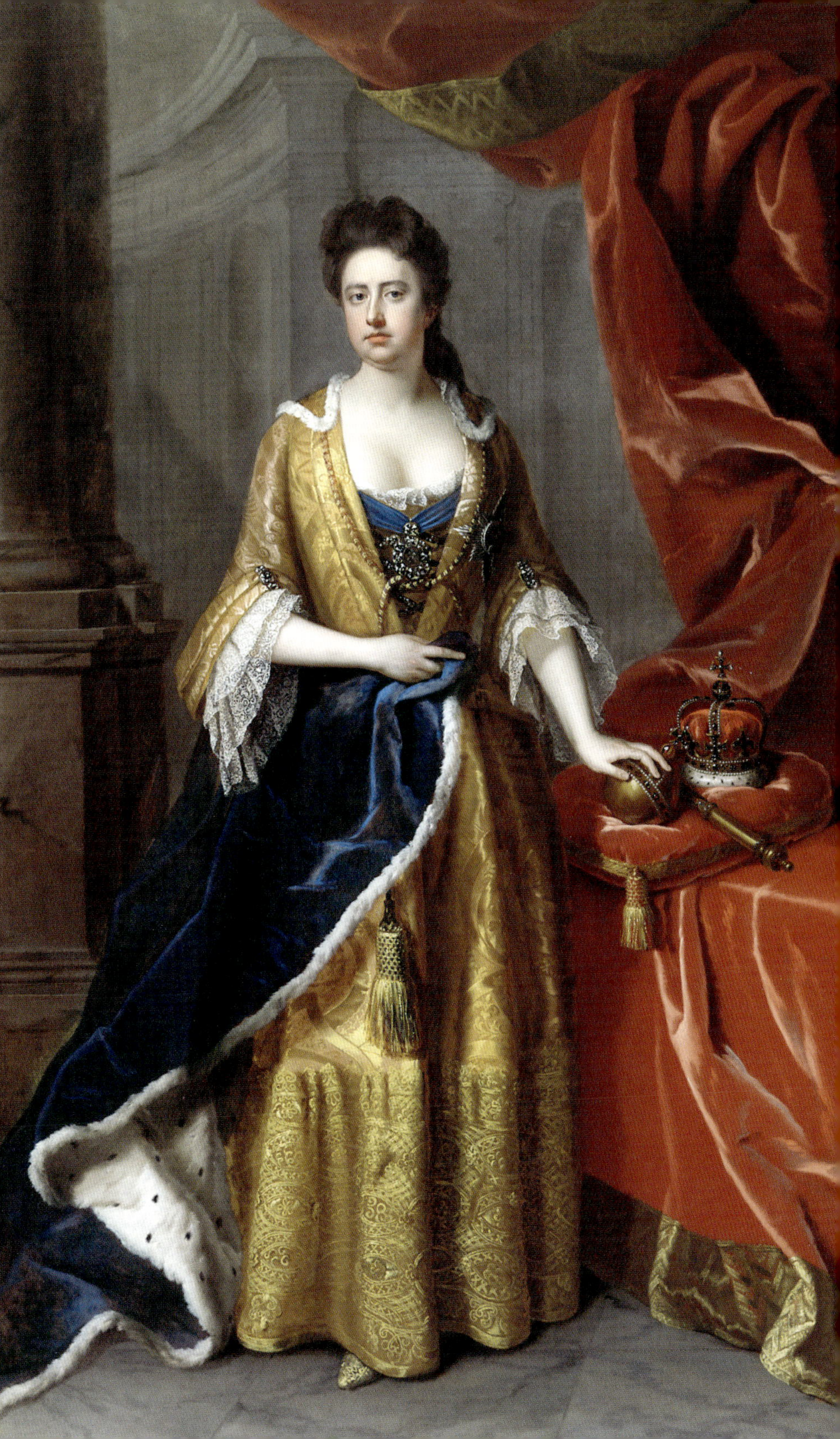

THE GEORGIANS

1714–1837

Previous spread (detail)
KING GEORGE IV
SIR THOMAS LAWRENCE, c.1814

Oil on canvas, 914 x 711mm
NPG 123

The Georgian era derives its name from the succession of four Hanoverian kings named George. Despite continuing religious tensions at home and a series of wars with France, under the Georges Britain became a world power, an industrial giant and a dynamic commercial society.

To guarantee the constitutional monarchy and the Protestant succession, as stipulated by the Act of Succession in 1701, Parliament invited George of Hanover, great-grandson of James I, to take the throne upon the death of Anne. He was crowned George I, and the Hanoverian dynasty replaced the Stuarts. George I spoke limited English and spent much of his reign in Hanover.

George I's son succeeded to the throne, becoming George II. His reign witnessed rapid financial growth and increasing political stability in Britain. George II was succeeded in 1760 by his grandson, George III. The new king was much beloved and was the first Hanoverian to be born and raised in Britain, speaking English as his primary language.

Next in line was George III's son, who was crowned George IV. He was renowned for his lack of self-restraint, his greed and his hedonism. On George IV's death, his younger brother became king, as William IV. He signed the Great Reform Act into law in 1832 – the first of a series of reforms that eventually led to the full enfranchisement of the British people. His death in 1837 brought the Georgian era to a close.

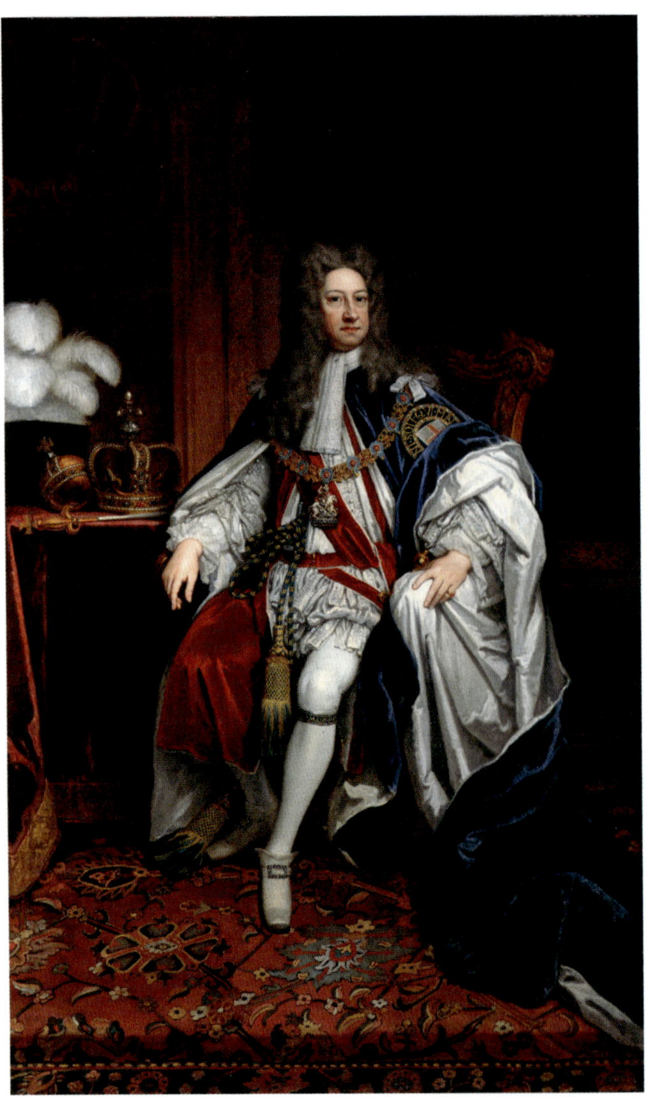

Georg Ludwig of Hanover was the great-grandson of James I through his mother Sophia, Electress of Hanover. He succeeded to the British throne as King George I (r.1714–27) on the death of the last Stuart monarch, Anne, under the terms of the Act of Settlement of 1701, which was designed to ensure a Protestant succession.

George spoke scant English and, as he continued to rule Hanover, he spent little time in Britain. George's accession had triggered unrest among the Jacobites, who supported the Catholic Stuart claim to the throne. Their first uprising to attempt to restore the Stuart dynasty was defeated in 1715.

Painted by Sir Godfrey Kneller, the most eminent portrait artist working in Britain at the time, this is one of many contemporary versions of George I's coronation portrait. The royal regalia and the richness of his surroundings convey his power and status rather than his personality.

[41]
KING GEORGE I
(1660–1727)
SIR GODFREY KNELLER, 1716, BASED ON A WORK OF 1714

Oil on canvas, 2470 x 1518mm
NPG 5174

George, Prince of Wales, the only son of George I and Sophia Dorothea of Celle, was born in 1683. He married the German princess Caroline of Brandenburg-Ansbach in 1705, and together they accompanied his father when he moved to London upon his accession. Discord between the king and his eldest son began in 1717 and the Prince and Princess of Wales withdrew from court. Their departure did not obstruct the succession, and following his father's death George acceded the throne as King George II (r.1727–60).

Despite successive wars with Catholic France and the king's frequent absences abroad, George II's reign witnessed increasing political stability and rapid financial growth. A Jacobite uprising in 1745 failed to restore the Stuart dynasty and they were decisively defeated at the Battle of Culloden in 1746.

It was also during George II's reign that the Hanoverians achieved a measure of popularity; indeed, the national anthem, 'God Save the King', was first performed to celebrate George II.

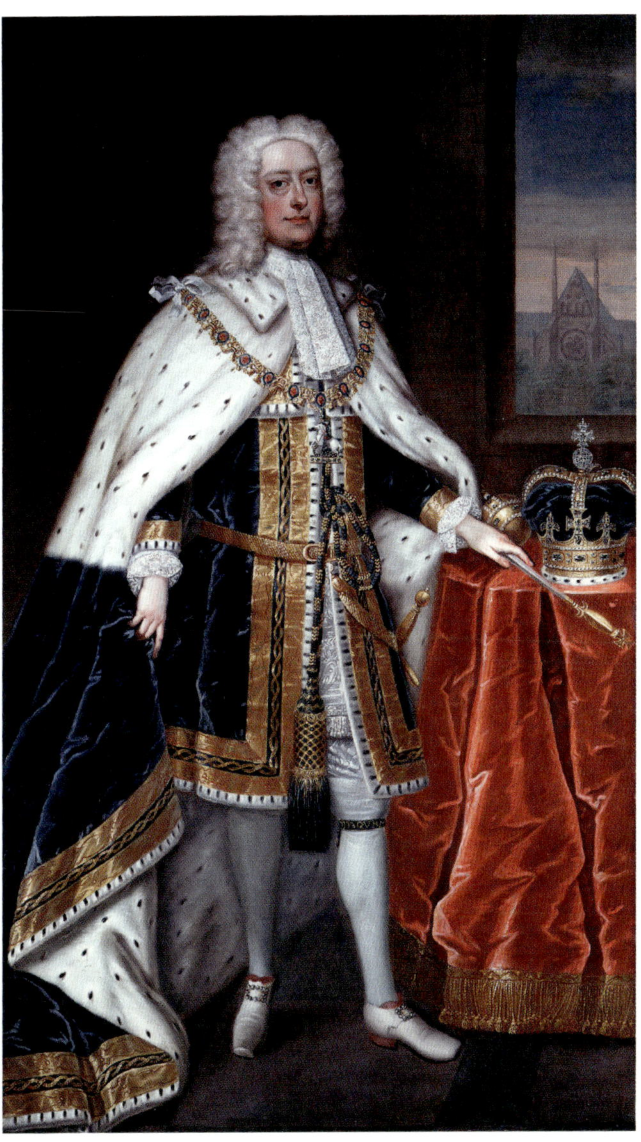

[42]
KING GEORGE II
(1683–1760)
STUDIO OF CHARLES JERVAS, c.1727

Oil on canvas, 2197 x 1283mm
NPG 368

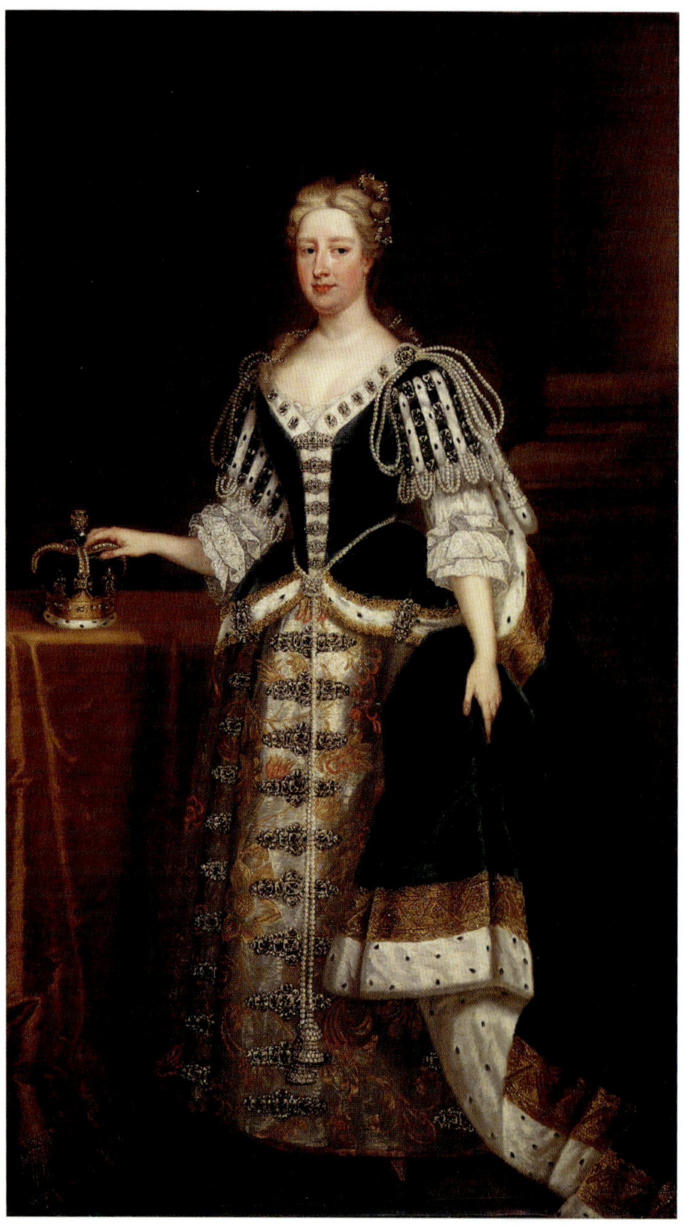

The German princess Caroline of Brandenburg-Ansbach was married to George II in 1705. She was the third and youngest daughter of John Frederick of Brandenburg-Ansbach, and his second wife, Eleanor of Saxe-Eisenach.

Caroline exercised more power than any queen consort since the Middle Ages. She served as queen regent during her husband's frequent absences abroad, and her political influence was key to the rise of Sir Robert Walpole, the first prime minister.

Together, George and Caroline had nine children, seven surviving beyond infancy. A rift grew between the parents and their son Frederick, Prince of Wales, repeating the dysfunctional relationship that the king had experienced with his own father. Caroline described her son as 'the greatest ass, and the greatest liar'. Frederick died suddenly in March 1751, leaving his son as heir to the throne.

[43]
CAROLINE OF BRANDENBURG-ANSBACH
(1683–1737)
CHARLES JERVAS, 1727

Oil on canvas, 2185 x 1276mm
NPG 369

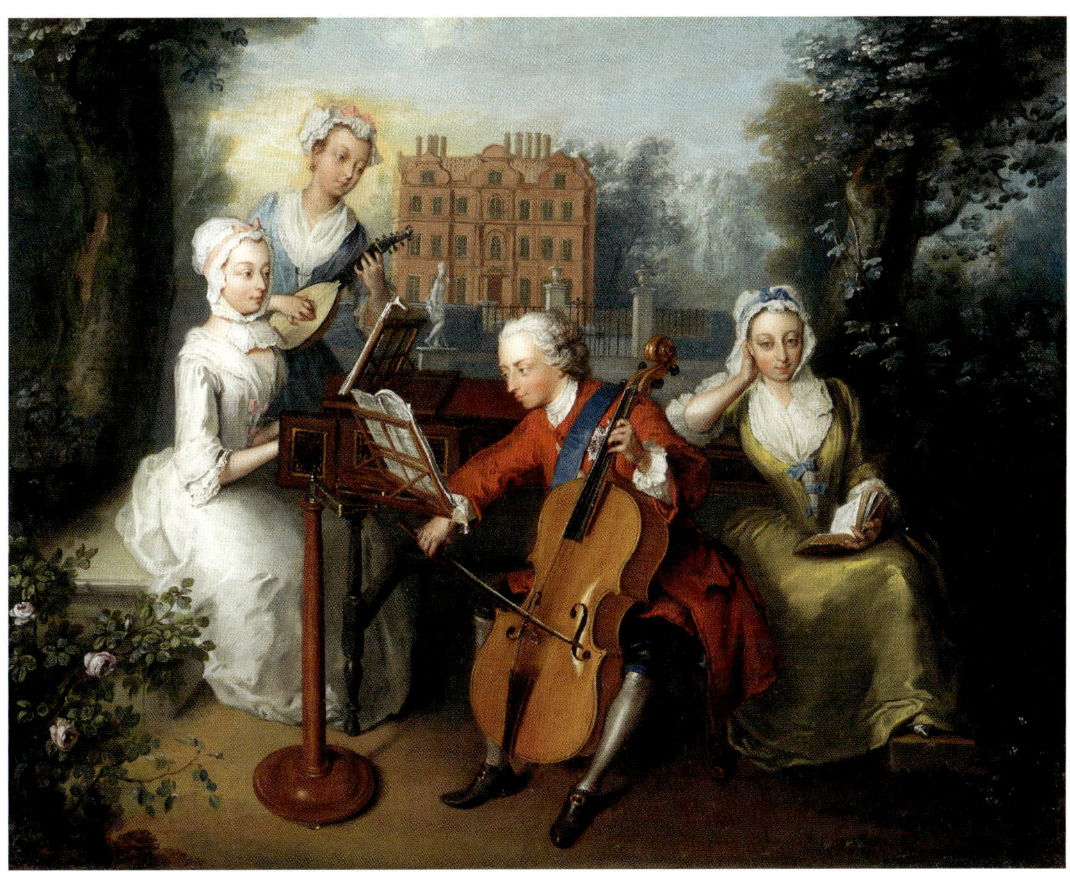

[44]
'THE MUSIC PARTY'
ANNE, PRINCESS ROYAL AND PRINCESS OF ORANGE (1709–59); PRINCESS CAROLINE (1713–57); FREDERICK, PRINCE OF WALES (1707–51); PRINCESS AMELIA (1711–86)

PHILIP MERCIER, 1733
Oil on canvas, 451 x 578mm
NPG 1556

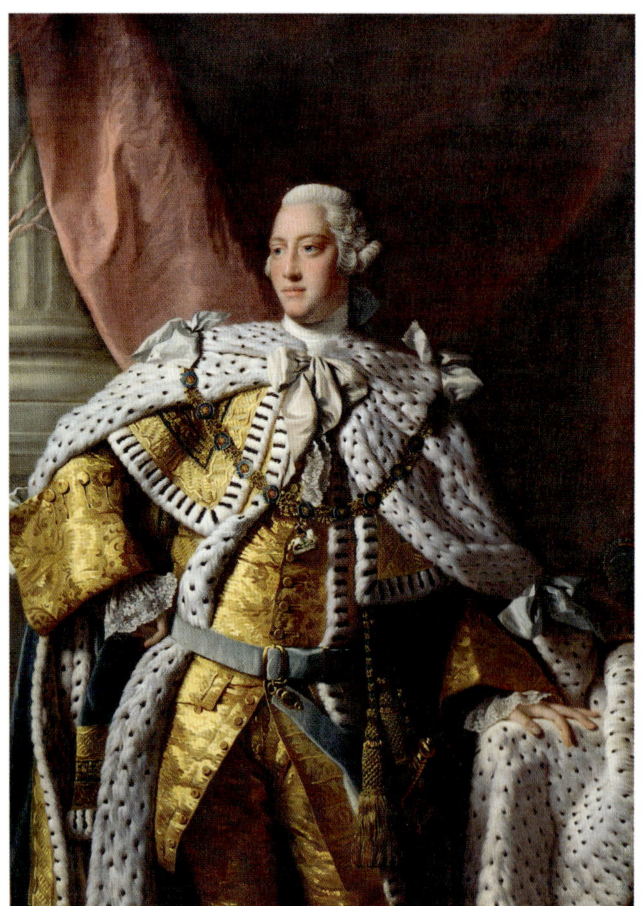

George was the grandson of George II and Caroline of Brandenburg-Ansbach. He succeeded his grandfather in October 1760, becoming King George III (r.1760–1820). He was more cultured and engaged in British life than his Hanoverian royal predecessors, and his fascination for agricultural improvement led to his popular nickname 'Farmer George'.

He married Charlotte of Mecklenburg-Strelitz, a German princess, in 1761. Crowned two weeks later, he reigned during a period of great cultural development, which included the establishment of the Royal Academy of Arts in 1768.

Today, George is mainly remembered for Britain's loss of the American colonies during his reign, and the long periods of debilitating illness that left him unable to rule. Though his illness began in 1788, George did not withdraw completely until 1811, when his eldest son became Prince Regent.

[45]
KING GEORGE III
(1738–1820)
STUDIO OF ALLAN RAMSAY, BASED ON A WORK OF 1761–62

Oil on canvas, 1473 x 1067mm
NPG 223

Charlotte of Mecklenburg-Strelitz was a German princess, the daughter of Charles of Mecklenburg-Stelitz and Elizabeth of Saxe-Hildburghausen. George III and Charlotte first met on their wedding day in 1761. Overcoming initial obstacles of language, they forged a strong and affectionate bond and had 15 children, of whom 13 survived into adulthood.

Charlotte lived up to the contemporary ideal of a queen. She was devoted to her husband and was an excellent host who rarely involved herself in politics. She surrounded herself with female intellectuals and was an important patron of art and science. During George's illness, Charlotte was of great support.

In this pair of portraits, they are wearing their matching gold and ermine coronation robes. Many of the studio versions of these pictures found their way to Britain's newly acquired colonial territories, where they represented the authority of the emerging British Empire.

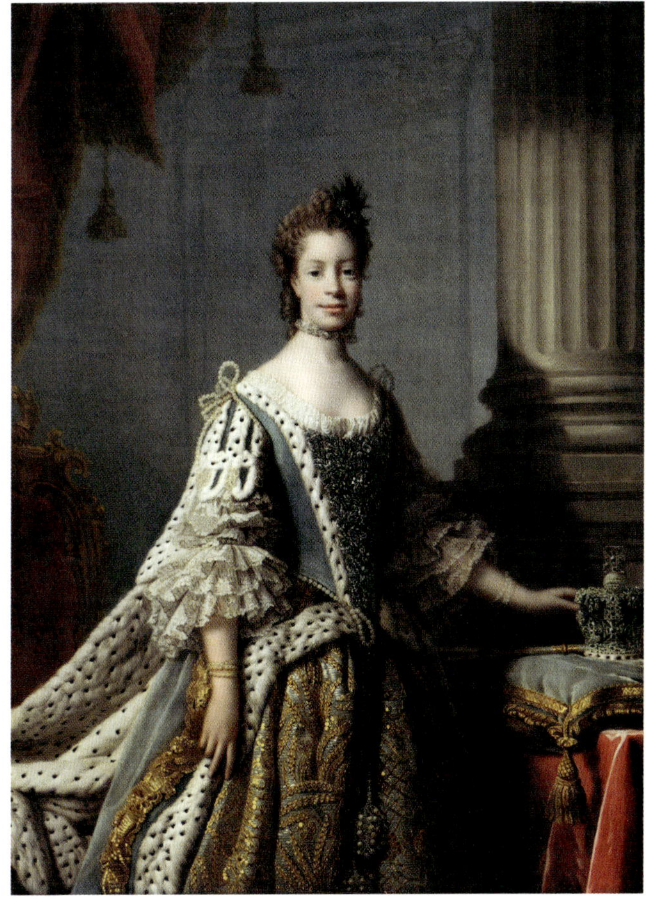

[46]
QUEEN CHARLOTTE OF MECKLENBURG-STRELITZ
(1744–1818)
STUDIO OF ALLAN RAMSAY, BASED ON A WORK OF 1761–62

Oil on canvas, 1480 x 1080mm
NPG 224

George (r.1820–30) was the eldest son of George III and Queen Charlotte. He was renowned for his lack of self-restraint, his greed and his hedonism, which increased, along with his spending power, as regent and then king.

In 1795, Parliament offered to pay off the prince's huge debts. In exchange, he agreed to a dynastic marriage with Caroline of Brunswick. He spent most of their marriage with other women, including Maria Fitzherbert who he had illegally married in secret before his marriage to Caroline. George's lifestyle and attempts to divorce Caroline led to him being widely vilified as decadent, a neglectful husband and a symbol of aristocratic corruption.

Like many of his predecessors, as the eldest son of the monarch, he sought to undermine the king by siding with his political opponents. When the king suffered a bout of illness in 1788, the prime minister, William Pitt, proposed a restricted regency to protect the king's interests. The king's recovery three months later ended the 'regency crisis'. Pitt's Regency Bill was revived, however, during the king's final illness. George was sworn regent in 1811, crowned king in 1820 and ruled until 1830.

[47]
KING GEORGE IV
(1762–1830)
AFTER SIR THOMAS LAWRENCE, c.1815,
BASED ON A WORK OF 1815

Oil on canvas, 2413 x 1549mm
NPG 2503

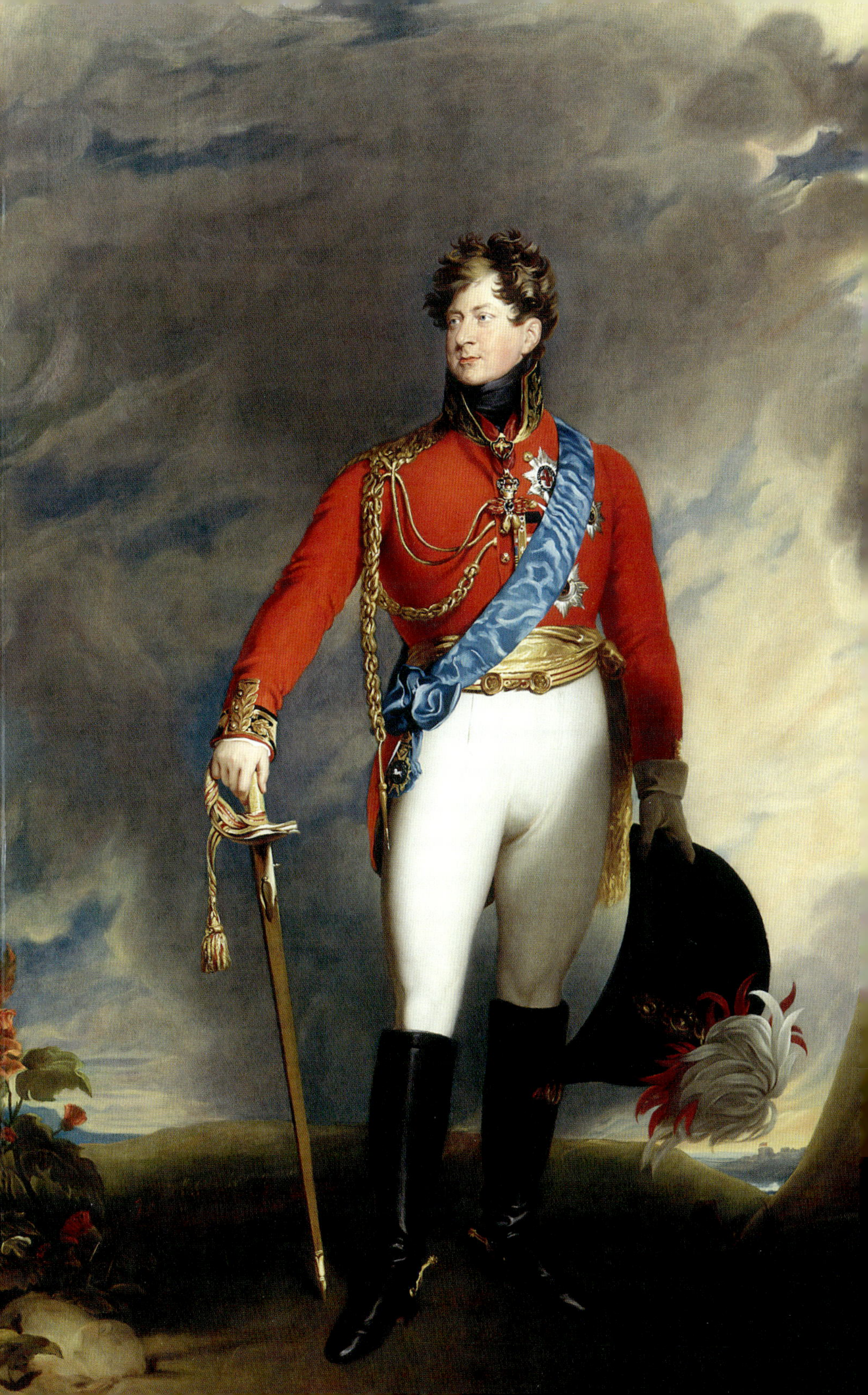

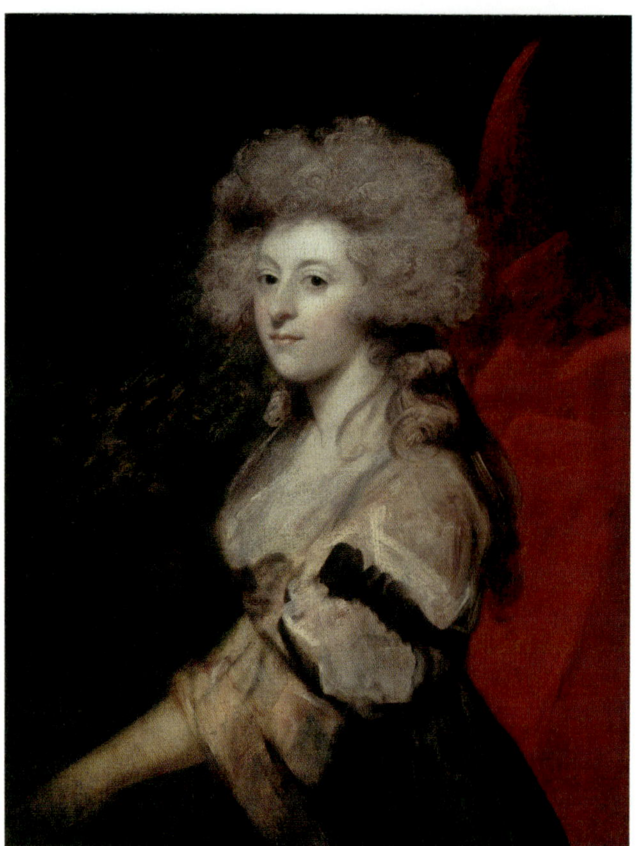

Maria Fitzherbert was a society beauty but, as a Catholic, she was an unsuitable match for the king's eldest son, George IV. That did not stop the love-struck Prince of Wales from pursuing her relentlessly after they met in 1784.

Maria resisted his advances until George staged a melodramatic suicide attempt to coerce her into marriage. This marriage was not only secret but it was also illegal, as members of the royal family could not marry without the king's approval.

Until 1805, Fitzherbert lived as the prince's wife-mistress. Despite his many other affairs, when George IV died in 1830, he was wearing a miniature portrait of Fitzherbert. It was buried with him.

[48]
MARIA FITZHERBERT
(1756–1837)
SIR JOSHUA REYNOLDS, c.1788

Oil on canvas, 914 x 711mm
NPG L162

Princess Caroline of Brunswick-Wolfenbüttel was the German first cousin of George IV. She and George were married in 1795 despite overtly disliking one another.

Once their daughter, Charlotte, was born in 1796, George went back to his secret wife, Maria Fitzherbert. Caroline repaid her husband's scorn by leading a life of defiant behaviour, developing an alternative court at her house in Blackheath and taking lovers as she travelled across Europe.

On her return to Britain, Caroline became 'the people's queen' and a figurehead for those agitating for rights for women and workers. She was refused admission to her husband's coronation at Westminster Abbey in 1821. She fell ill and died just three weeks later.

Thomas Lawrence's portrait captures Caroline in a defiant mood after her separation from George. Her wedding ring is in shadow and she poses with a bust of her father rather than her husband.

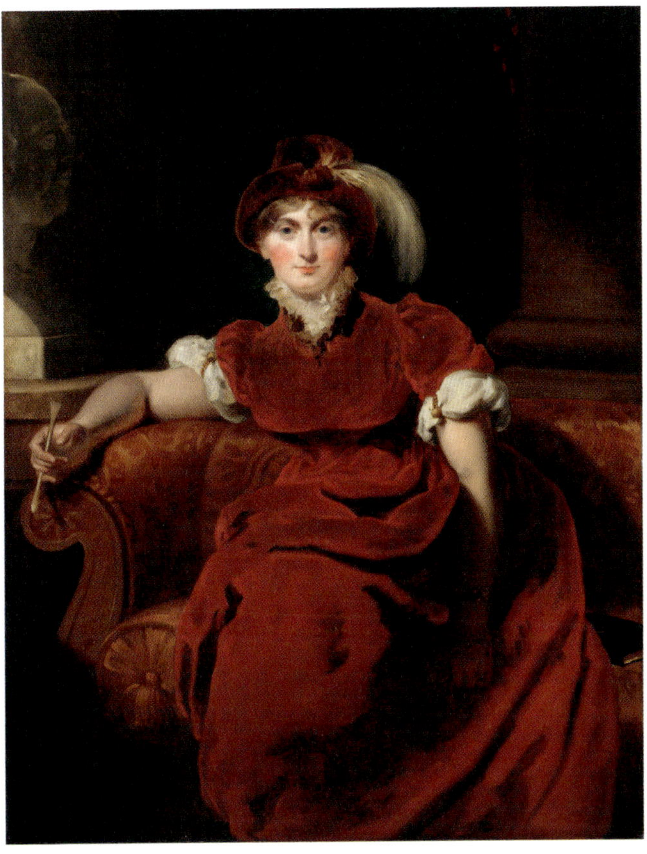

[49]
PRINCESS CAROLINE OF BRUNSWICK-WOLFENBÜTTEL
(1768–1821)
SIR THOMAS LAWRENCE, 1804

Oil on canvas, 1403 x 1118mm
NPG 244

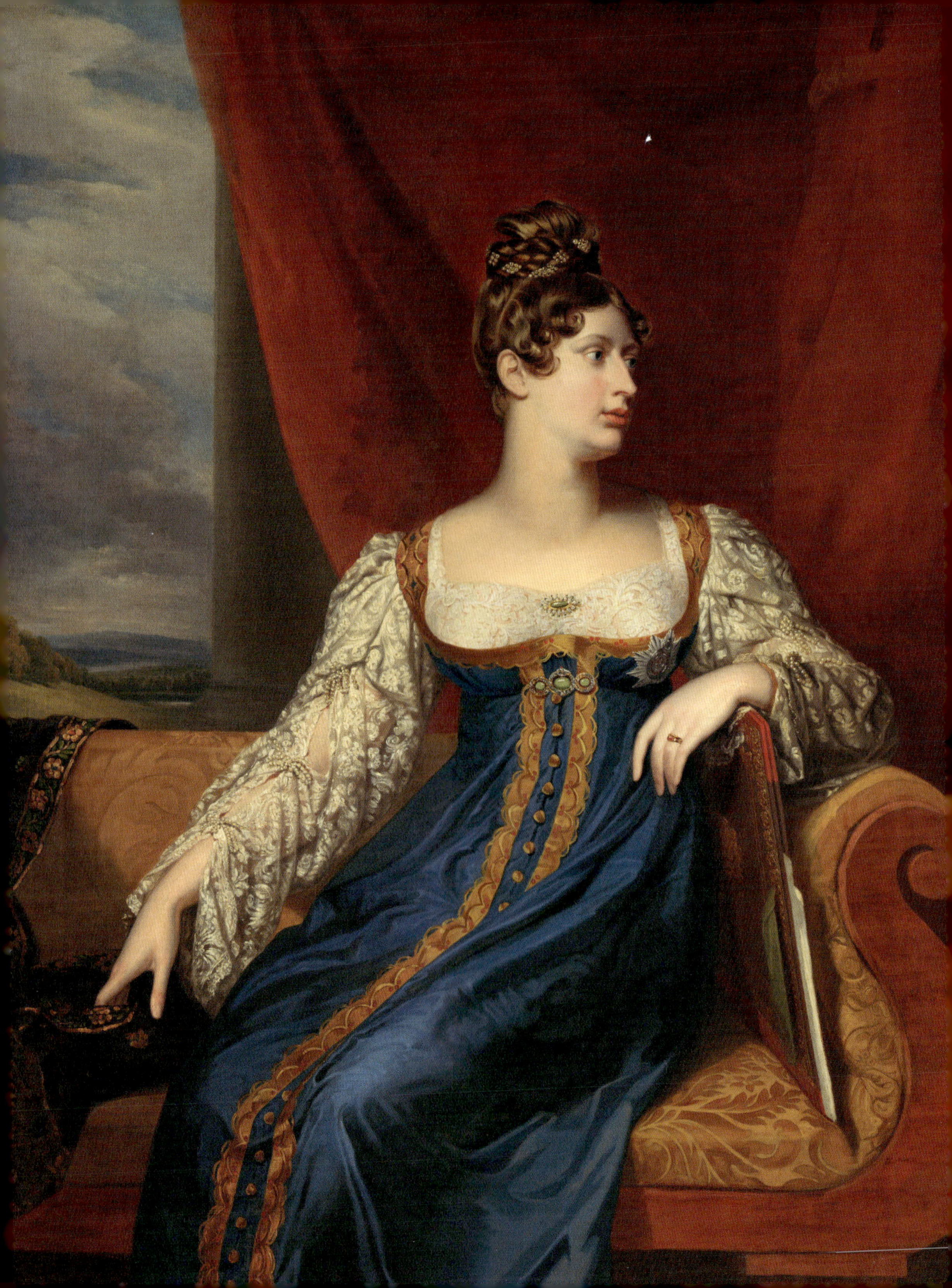

Princess Charlotte of Wales was the daughter of George IV and Caroline of Brunswick. Charlotte's parents separated a few months after her birth. She was brought up by governesses and saw little of her mother. Charlotte resisted her father's pressure to marry the Prince of Orange and instead fell in love with Prince Leopold of Saxe-Coburg. They were married in 1816.

Public opinion despaired at the morality of her father's generation of royals, and all hopes were placed on Princess Charlotte coming to the throne. This was not to happen. She died in childbirth in 1817, to great public lament. There then followed a succession crisis as George III had no other legitimate grandchildren until the birth of Victoria in 1819.

[50]
PRINCESS CHARLOTTE OF WALES
(1796–1817)
GEORGE DAWE, 1817

Oil on canvas, 1397 x 1080mm
NPG 51

William (r.1830–37) was the third son of George III and Queen Charlotte. He scandalised society by living with the actress Dorothy Jordan for 20 years. The couple had ten illegitimate children before he left her to find an official bride.

The pressure to marry and produce a legitimate heir was increased by the death of Princess Charlotte in 1817. He married Princess Adelaide of Saxe-Meiningen the following year but the couple left no heirs.

He became King William IV on the death of his elder brother George IV, and in 1832 signed the Great Reform Act, which was a major step in the slow enfranchisement of the British people.

Five years later, he died peacefully of pneumonia with his head resting on Adelaide's shoulder.

This portrait shows William about 30 years before he became king, when he was an admiral in the Royal Navy. He wears his naval uniform with the sash, garter and star of the Order of the Garter.

[51]
KING WILLIAM IV
(1765–1837)
SIR MARTIN ARCHER SHEE, c.1800

Oil on canvas, 2210 x 1499mm
NPG 2199

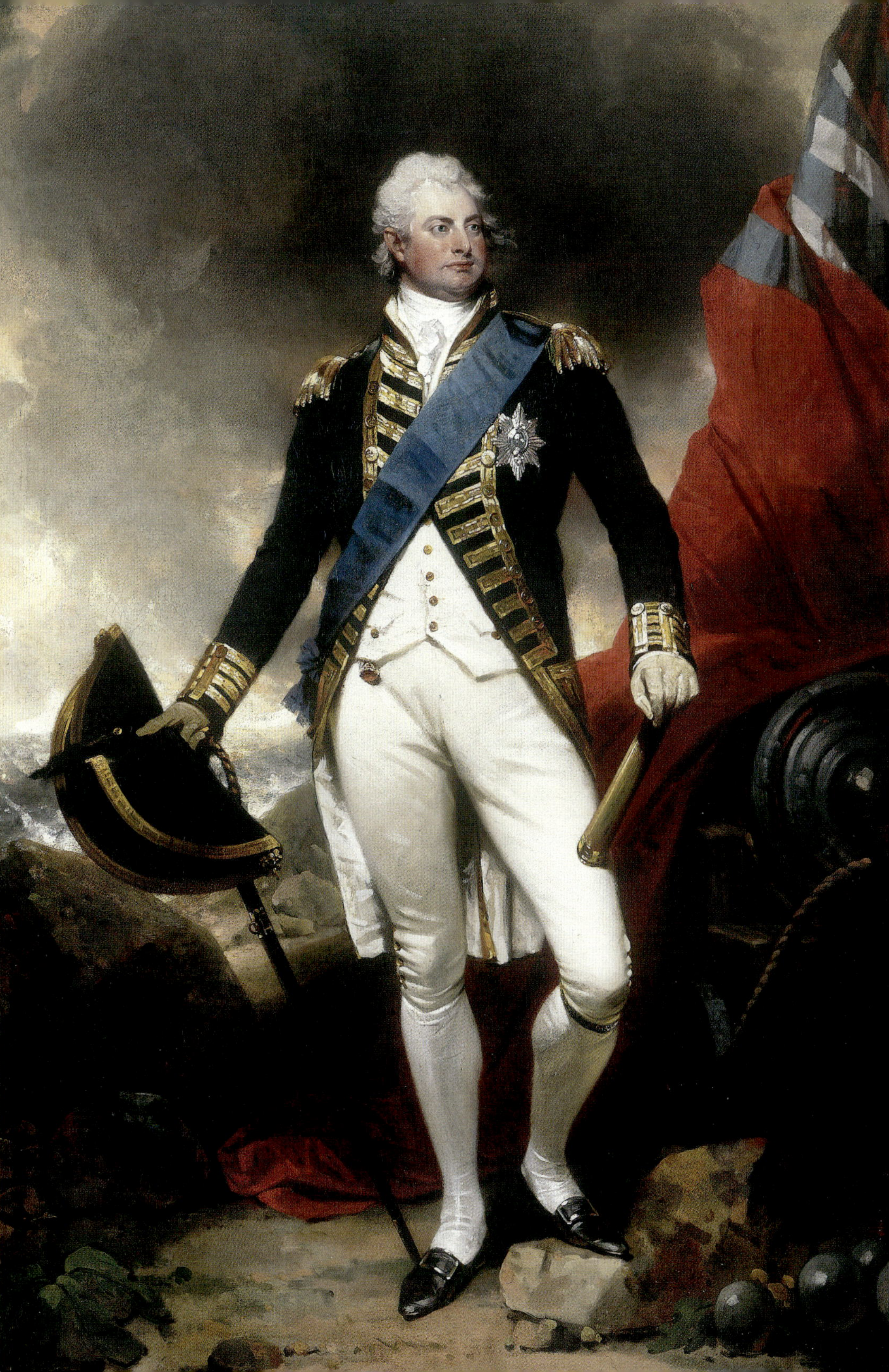

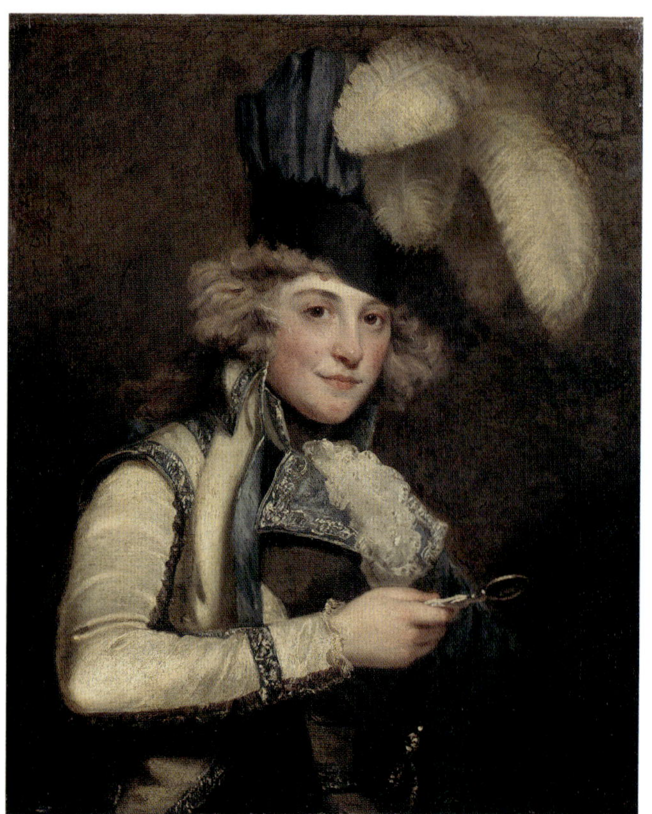

Dorothy Jordan was the leading comic actress of her day, known for roles that required her to cross-dress as a man, which was titillating for eighteenth-century audiences. Before he acceded the throne, William IV had a long-term relationship with Dorothy. She is shown here in the costume of a young soldier, painted in the first year of her relationship with William.

Endless press attention fed the public obsession with her life with William. They lived together for 20 years, having ten illegitimate children. She continued to act, often paying his gambling debts from her income.

In 1811, William's debts and the pressure to make an advantageous and official marriage forced him to end the relationship. Jordan died alone in France, where she fled to escape her own debts.

[52]
DOROTHY JORDAN
(1761–1816)
JOHN HOPPNER, 1791

Oil on canvas, 749 x 622mm
NPG 7041

Princess Adelaide of Saxe-Meiningen was born in Germany. She married William in 1818 and became queen consort when he acceded the throne in 1830. The couple hoped to conceive an heir, but Adelaide suffered several miscarriages and their two children did not survive beyond infancy. Adelaide found solace in mothering William's children from his relationship with Dorothy Jordan.

Adelaide donated generously to charities that supported women and orphans. This was an expression of her kindness and it also gave her a public role. Adelaide's legacy can be seen in the charitable patronage of many members of the royal family today.

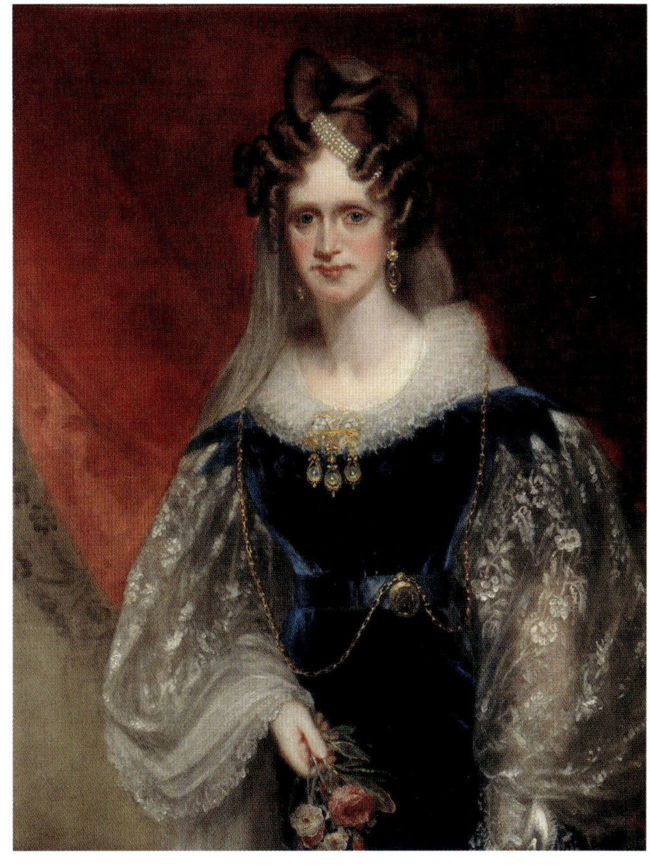

[53]
QUEEN ADELAIDE OF SAXE-MEININGEN
(1792–1849)
UNKNOWN ARTIST AFTER A PORTRAIT BY SIR WILLIAM BEECHEY, c.1831

Oil on canvas, 914 x 705mm
NPG 1533

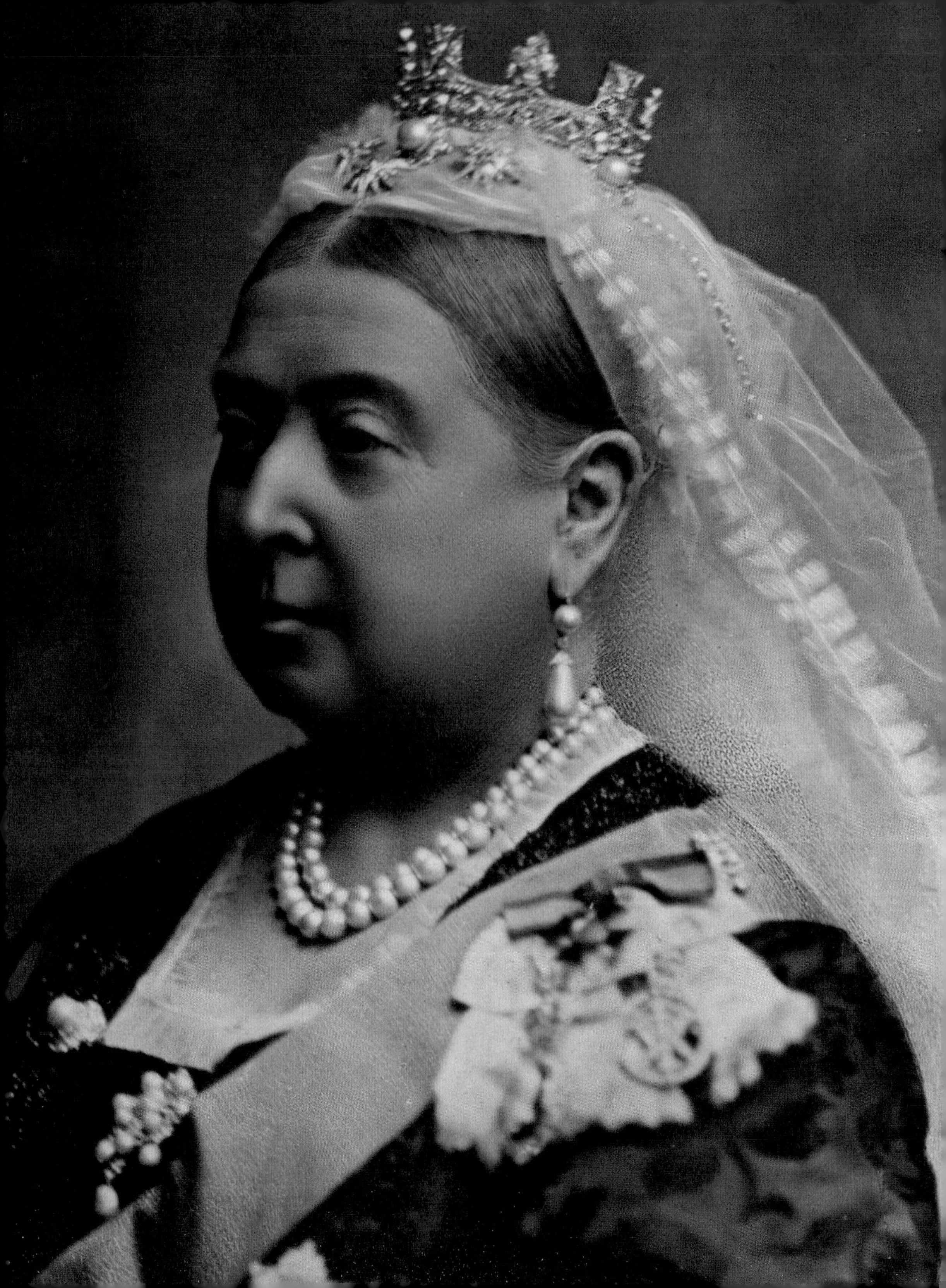

THE VICTORIANS

1837–1910

Previous spread (detail)
QUEEN VICTORIA
LAFAYETTE, 1887

Gelatin silver print, 143 x 95mm
NPG Ax26453

Victoria's coronation in 1838 was hailed as a new era for Britain. She was just 18 when she ascended the throne, following the death of her uncle William IV. By virtue of her youth and gender, Victoria was perceived as untainted by the familial disputes and debaucheries that had characterised the reigns of her Georgian predecessors.

In portraits of the queen, artists attempted to reconcile the contradictory realities of her public power with traditional female virtues. One of the most crucial developments in image making occurred during Victoria's reign: the invention of photography. Both the queen and her consort, Prince Albert, sat for numerous photographic portraits and were keen patrons of this new technology.

The Victorian period bore witness to many other major developments in science, technology and philosophy, which continue to shape the way we live today. Under Victoria, Britain's empire became the largest in the world, including India, Canada, Australia and territories in Africa and Southeast Asia. As the empire grew, Britain became extremely wealthy at the expense of the countries and peoples it colonised.

After Victoria's death in 1901, her eldest son was crowned as Edward VII. Known as the Edwardian period, his rule coincided with increased public attention on the campaign for women's suffrage and developments in welfare legislation.

William IV and Adelaide of Saxe-Meiningen's childless marriage meant that, following William's death, the crown passed to his niece, Queen Victoria (r.1837–1901).

Victoria was just 18 when she came to the throne. Her coronation in 1838 was hailed as a new era for Britain. Victoria was greeted with enthusiasm because she was untainted by the debauchery of her father's generation. A few years after becoming queen she married her cousin, Prince Albert of Saxe-Coburg and Gotha.

Through wars and conquests, Britain's colonies and interests abroad were formally transformed into an empire with Victoria at its head. Although royal power was declining, she held influence over the foreign and domestic policies of the governments she oversaw.

Victoria was utterly devastated by the premature death of her husband, Albert, in 1861. She went into a period of deep mourning that extended beyond the year that was customary for Victorian widows, withdrawing from public life until 1868. Her 63-year reign was longer than any previous British monarch.

Victoria's coronation portrait highlights the crown and sceptre, symbols of royal authority.

[54]
QUEEN VICTORIA
(1819–1901)
REPLICA BY SIR GEORGE HAYTER, 1863,
BASED ON A WORK OF 1838

Oil on canvas, 2858 x 1790mm
NPG 1250

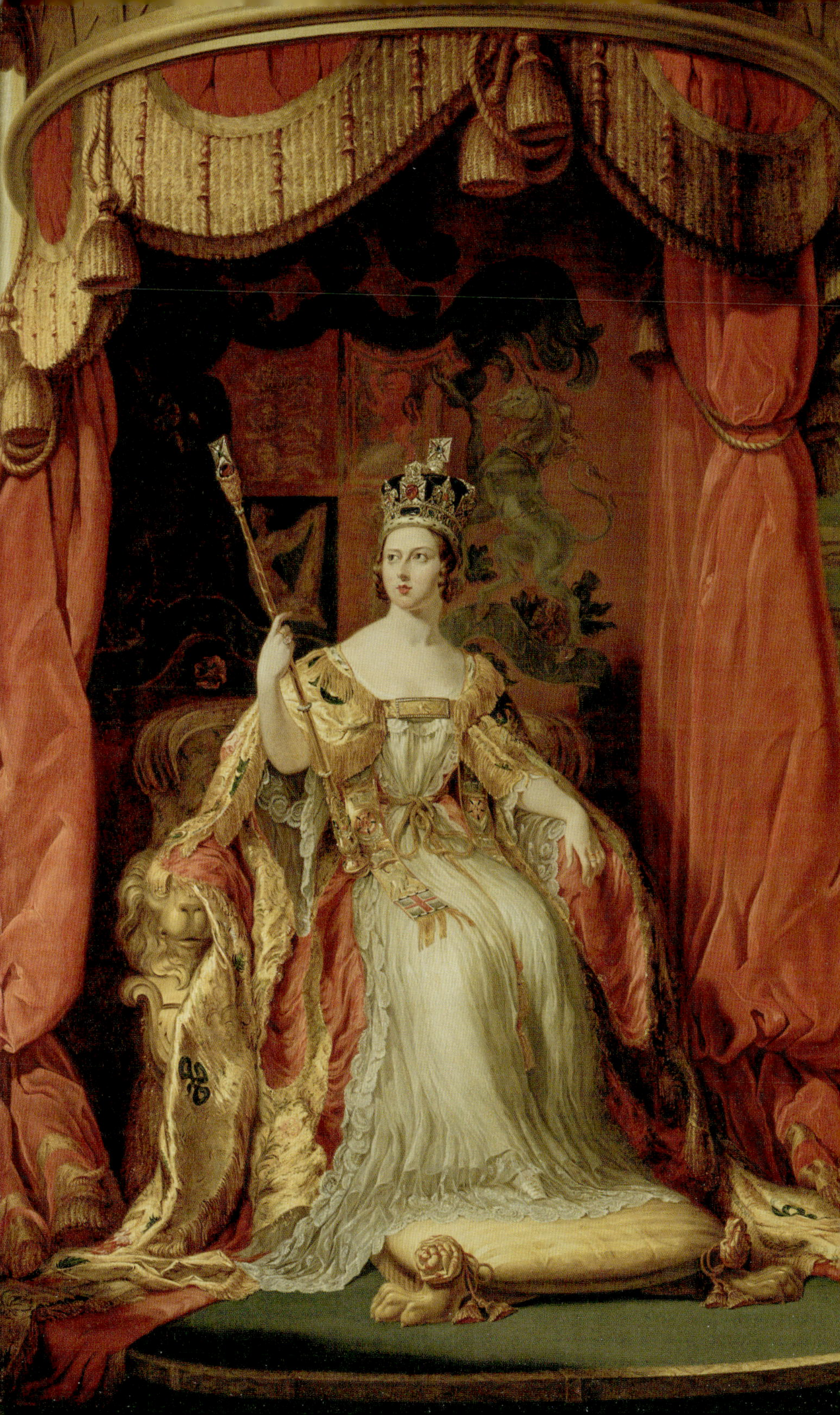

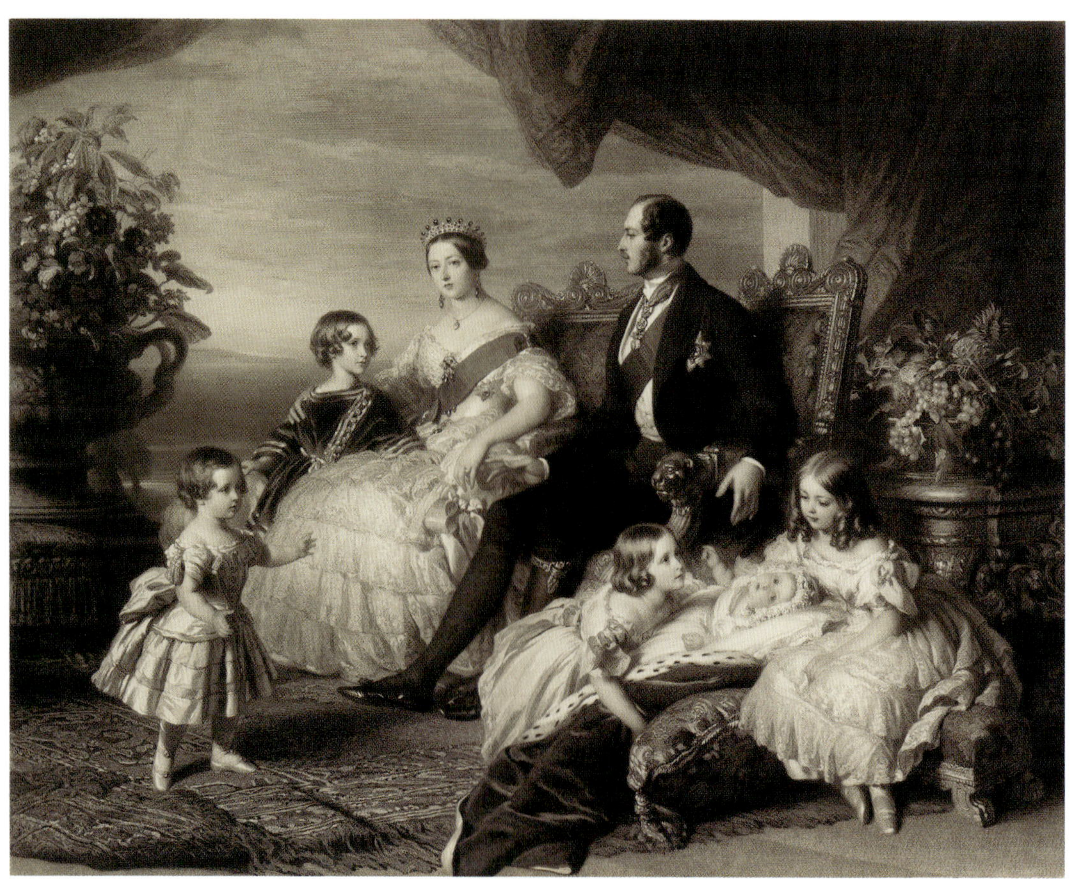

[55]
QUEEN VICTORIA, THE PRINCE CONSORT AND FAMILY
PRINCE ALFRED (1844–1900); KING EDWARD VII (1841–1910); QUEEN VICTORIA (1819–1901); PRINCE ALBERT OF SAXE-COBURG AND GOTHA (1819–61); PRINCESS ALICE (1843–78); PRINCESS HELENA (1846–1923); VICTORIA, EMPRESS OF GERMANY AND QUEEN OF PRUSSIA (1840–1901)

SAMUEL COUSINS, AFTER FRANZ XAVER WINTERHALTER, PUBLISHED 1853
Mixed-method engraving, 738 x 889mm
NPG D48098

Prince Albert of Saxe-Coburg and Gotha married Queen Victoria in 1840 and was given the title Prince Consort in 1857. They had nine children. While Victoria reigned as sovereign over the country, the couple adopted more conventional gender roles within the home. The idea of a traditional, patriarchal and morally upstanding royal family had a profound influence on social norms.

As consort, Prince Albert had no political power but was influential as a patron of the arts, taking a lead in organising the major British cultural event of the century: the Great Exhibition of 1851.

In 1861, Albert died of typhoid at the age of 42. Following his death, Victoria commissioned numerous posthumous portraits and initiated a programme of public commemoration, including the Royal Albert Hall and Albert Memorial in London. Victoria commissioned this portrait for the National Portrait Gallery in 1866.

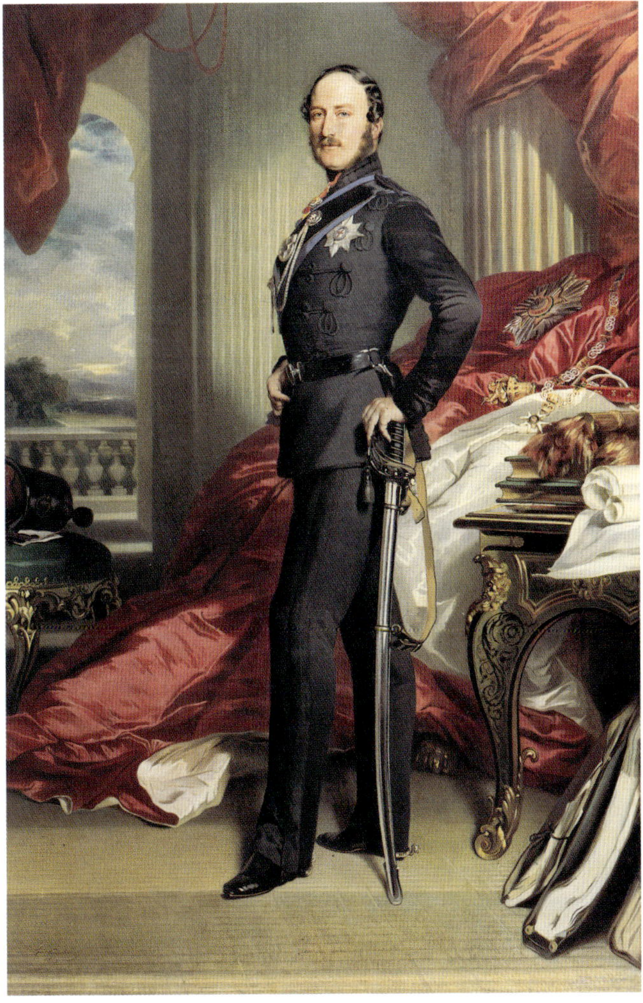

[56]
PRINCE ALBERT OF SAXE-COBURG AND GOTHA
REPLICA BY FRANZ XAVER WINTERHALTER, 1867, BASED ON A WORK OF 1859

Oil on canvas, 2413 x 1568mm
NPG 237

Edward was the eldest son of Queen Victoria and Prince Albert. In 1863, Edward married Alexandra of Denmark and they went on to have six children.

Following the death of Victoria, he became King Edward VII (r.1901–10). By the time he came to the throne, numerous technological innovations had transformed everyday life: the steam train, bicycle and motor car had replaced horse-drawn transport; candles and oil lamps had given way to gas lights and then electricity; and postal services had been supplemented by the telegraph and telephone. Edward loved sport, high living and novelty but, unlike his parents, had little interest in the visual arts.

Sir Luke Fildes's coronation portrait is laden with the traditional regalia and was given to the National Portrait Gallery by his son, George V, in 1912.

[57]
KING EDWARD VII
(1841–1910)
REPLICA BY SIR LUKE FILDES, c.1902–12,
BASED ON A WORK OF 1902

Oil on canvas, 2756 x 1803mm
NPG 1691

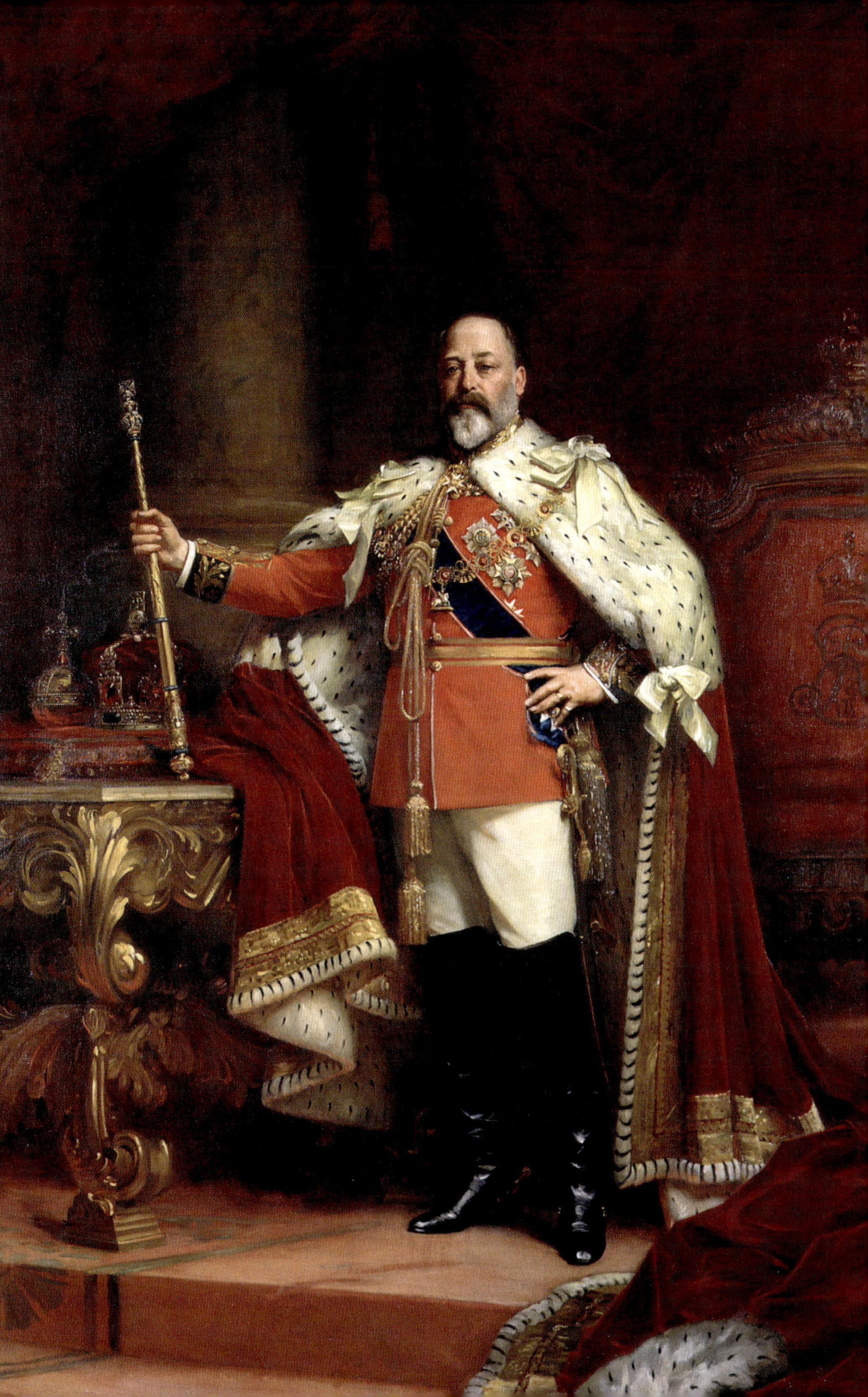

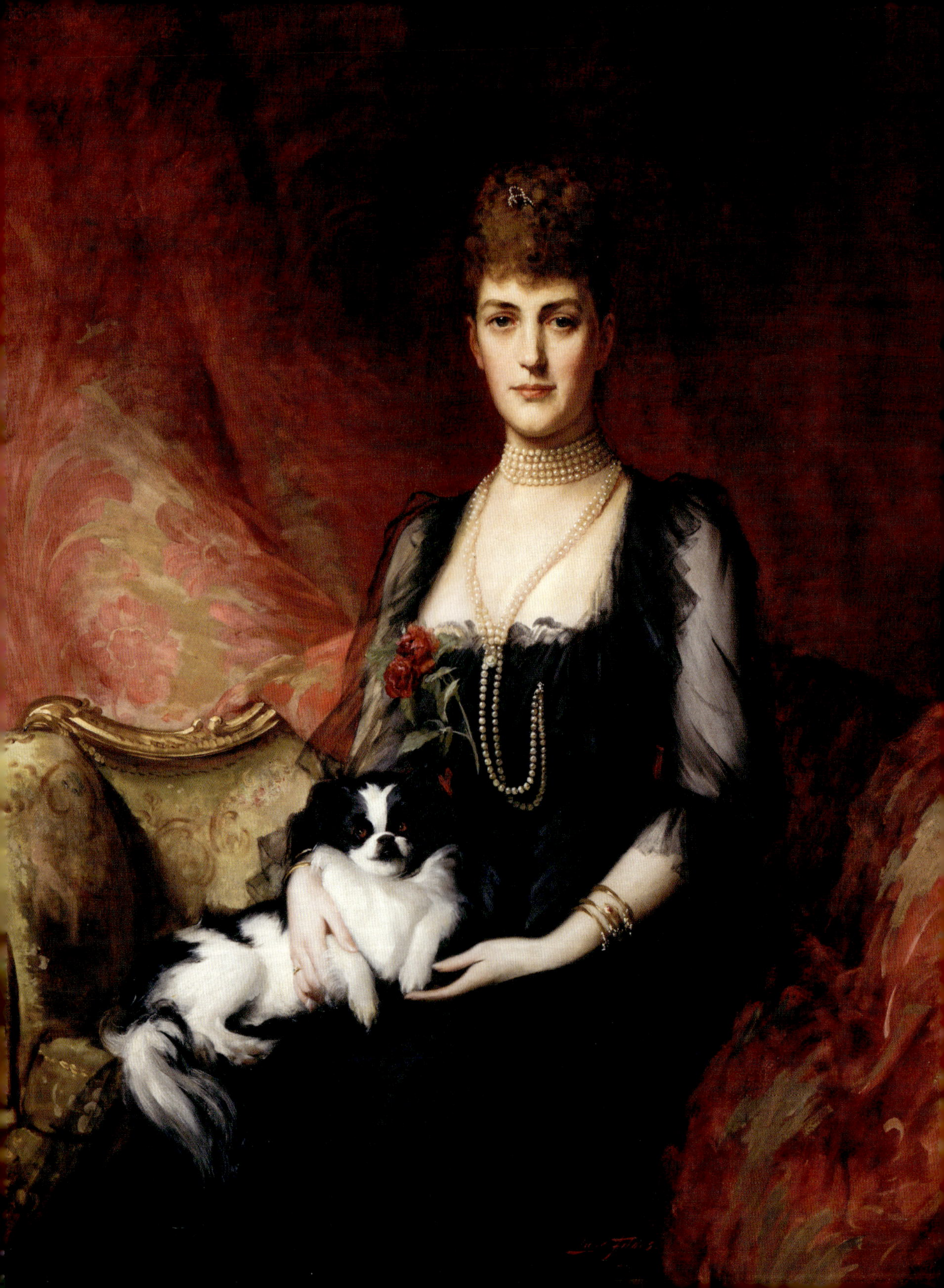

Princess Alexandra was the eldest daughter of Christian IX of Denmark and Louise of Hesse-Cassel. In 1863 she married Edward VII when he was Prince of Wales. It was hoped that Alexandra would curb Edward's wayward behaviour. When Queen Victoria died in 1901, Alexandra became queen consort. She became an important public figure and was widely respected for her commitment to her royal duties.

The queen consort founded the Royal Army Nursing Corps in 1902 and initiated the annual Alexandra Rose Day in aid of hospitals in 1912.

Alexandra's son, George V, commissioned this portrait and presented it to the National Portrait Gallery. The Japanese Chin dog is thought to be Alexandra's favourite pet, Punch.

[58]
QUEEN ALEXANDRA
(1844–1925)
AFTER SIR LUKE FILDES, 1920,
BASED ON A WORK OF 1894

Oil on canvas, 1283 x 1029mm
NPG 1889

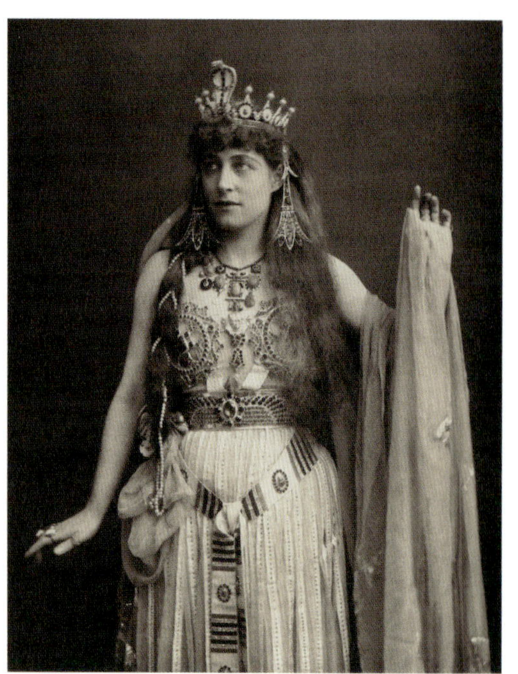

[59]
LILLIE LANGTRY
(1853–1929)
W. & D. DOWNEY, 1891

Photogravure, 233 x 184mm
NPG x17963

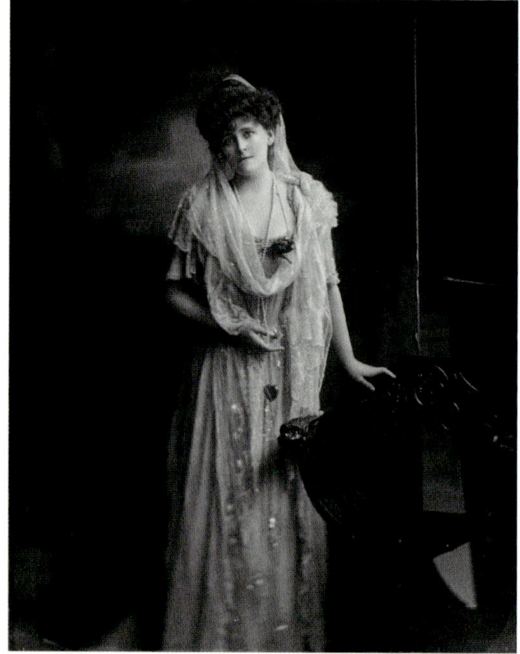

[60]
FRANCES EVELYN ('DAISY') GREVILLE, COUNTESS OF WARWICK
(1861–1938)
H. WALTER BARNETT, 1902

Whole-plate glass negative
NPG x81485

Edward VII's promiscuous behaviour recalled that of his Hanoverian great-uncles. His mother, Victoria, partly blamed Prince Albert's early death on the worry and stress caused by Edward's affairs. This resulted in a level of tension between the mother and son which was never healed.

Daisy, Countess of Warwick, and the actress Lillie Langtry were just two of Edward's most famous mistresses, but Alice Keppel was the last and most enduring. She became an accepted and visible presence in the royal entourage and was quietly tolerated by Queen Alexandra.

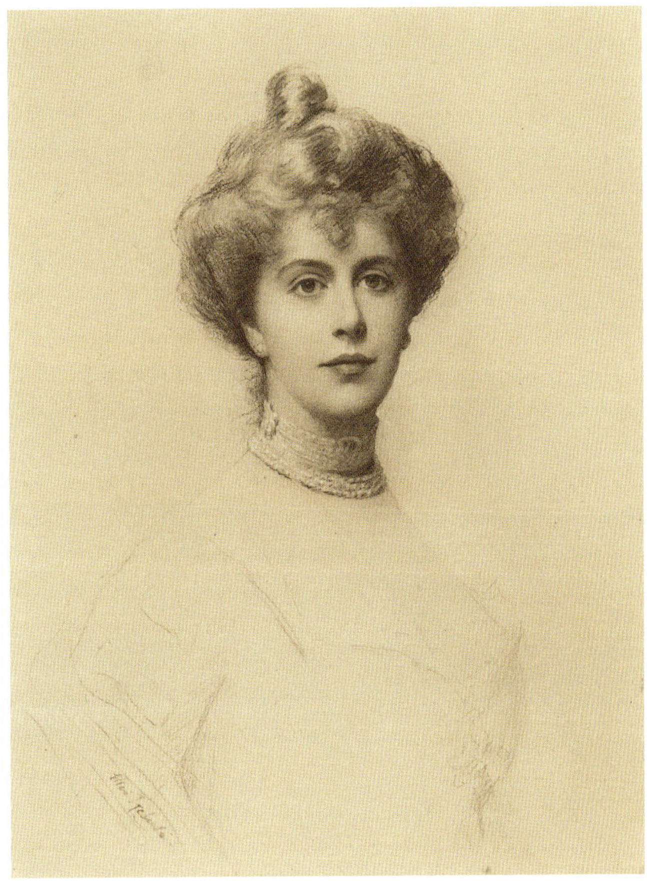

[61]
ALICE KEPPEL
(1868–1947)
FREDERICK JOHN JENKINS, AFTER ELLIS WILLIAM ROBERTS, c.1900–10

Photogravure, 279 x 203mm
NPG D8115

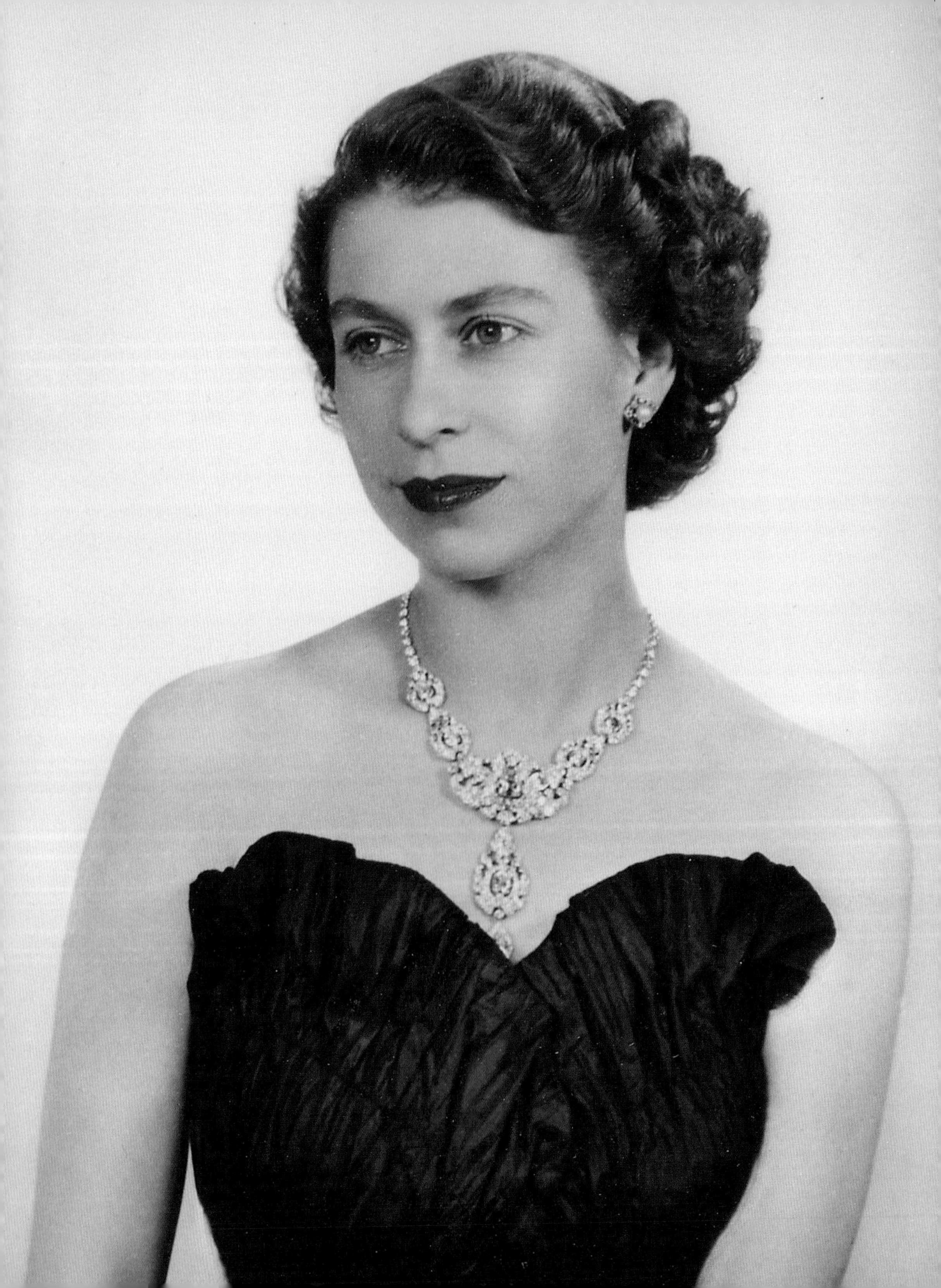

THE WINDSORS

1910–

Previous spread (detail)
QUEEN ELIZABETH II
DOROTHY WILDING, 1952

Gelatin silver print on tissue and card mount, 290 x 215mm
NPG P870(5)

When George V became king in 1910, he faced numerous challenges, most significantly the mounting tensions and crises leading to the First World War. In the context of hostilities between Great Britain and Germany, the Royal family's German connections and name Saxe-Coburg and Gotha, inherited from Prince Albert, were problematic. In 1917, George V changed the royal family's name to Windsor. At a time when ruling dynasties were being swept away by revolution, the British monarchy remained relatively stable.

This changed in 1936 when George V's eldest son, Edward VIII, abdicated after reigning for less than a year. He wanted to marry Wallis Simpson who was considered an unsuitable queen as she had twice been divorced. After the abdication, the throne passed to Edward's more serious and shy brother George VI. He became a respected statesman during his 16 years as king. After the Second World War, he presided over major changes at home and abroad, including the foundation of the National Health Service in 1948, and the beginning of the dismantling of the British Empire.

The accession of Elizabeth II in 1952 was hailed as the beginning of a new Elizabethan age. Much of the imagery devised for her coronation drew on Tudor paintings and heraldry, and brightened an otherwise austere post-war period. Elizabeth II ruled longer than any monarch in British history. When her son acceded the throne as King Charles III in 2022, he was the longest-waiting heir apparent in the history of the United Kingdom.

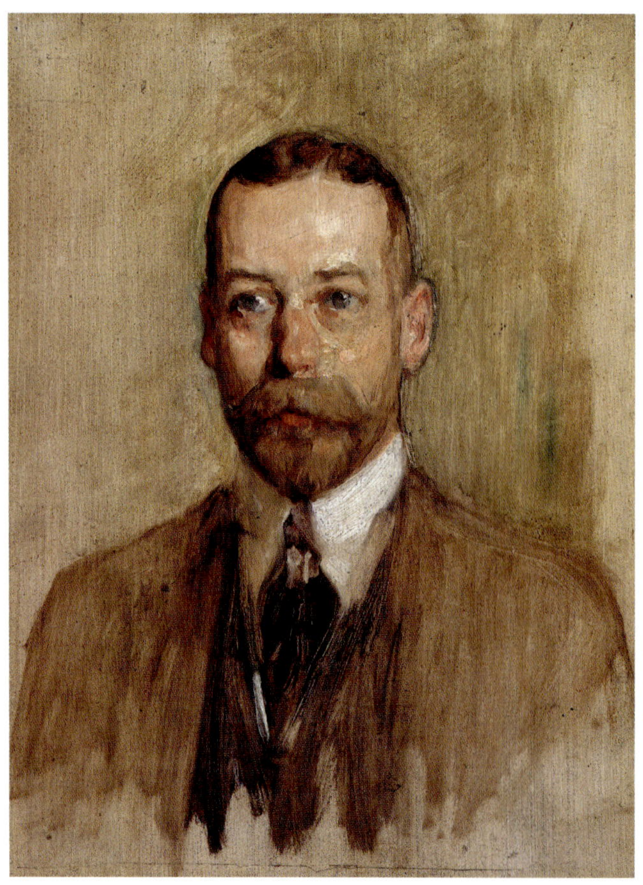

As the second son, George had not expected to become king, but the death of his elder brother Prince Albert in 1892 made him heir to the throne.

Upon the death of his father Edward VII in 1910, he became King George V (r.1910–36). In response to the anti-German feeling during the First World War, George changed the royal family name from Saxe-Coburg and Gotha to Windsor.

His personal experience as a naval commander in the 1890s – he wore naval uniform for public engagements throughout the war – endeared him to the wartime public.

Continually popular, the king held a great sense of duty towards Parliament and the country. George celebrated his Silver Jubilee just a year before his death in 1936.

[62]
KING GEORGE V
(1865–1936)
SOLOMON JOSEPH SOLOMON, 1914

Oil on panel, 298 x 244mm
NPG 5423

Princess Mary of Teck married George in 1893. They were happily married and had six children: Edward, Albert (later George VI), Mary, Henry, George and John. Mary became queen consort in 1910 and worked to promote charitable causes.

Mary, George and the wider royal family actively participated in the First World War. Mary boosted morale by visiting people affected by the conflict and formed the Queen's Work for Women Fund, which provided employment for women as part of the National Relief Fund. The contribution of British women to the war effort was instrumental to the first women winning the right to vote in 1918.

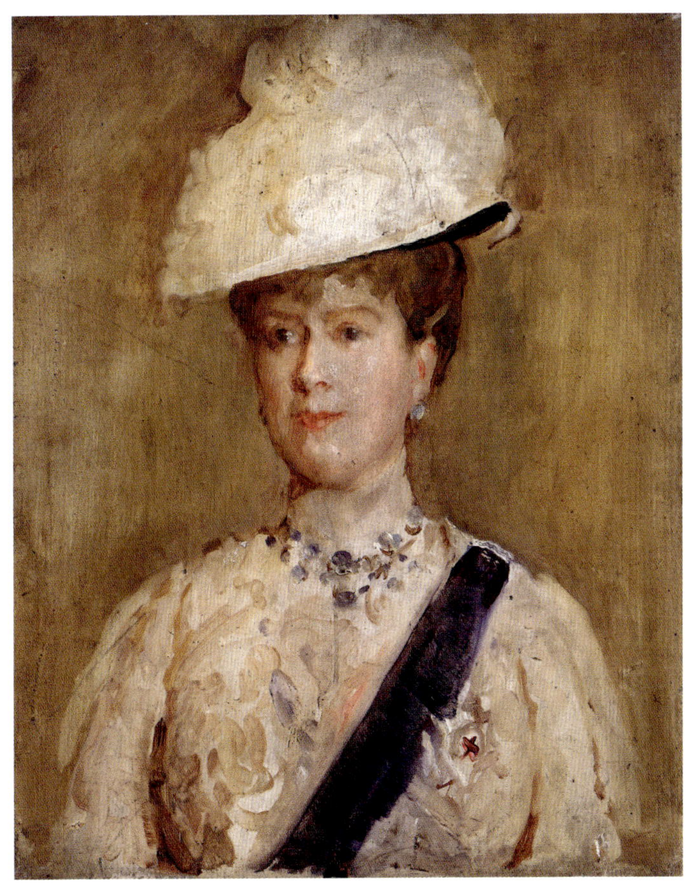

[63]
QUEEN MARY
(1867–1953)
SOLOMON JOSEPH SOLOMON, 1914

Oil on panel, 406 x 327mm
NPG 5424

This grand portrait shows the family of George V posed in the White Drawing Room at Buckingham Palace.

The Belfast-born artist John Lavery painted the portrait just a few months before the outbreak of the First World War. The queen and princess are seated, and appear more passive than the king and prince who are standing. This composition reflects traditional gender roles, but was painted at a time when women's role in society was being actively challenged by the suffrage movement.

The king is dressed in military uniform to signify duty and service to the nation. In this turbulent era, the serenity of Lavery's portrayal of a confident royal family may have reassured viewers. However, just two decades later, Prince Edward – the boy here – disrupted the stability of the royal family when, as Edward VIII, he abdicated.

[64]
'THE ROYAL FAMILY AT BUCKINGHAM PALACE, 1913'
KING GEORGE V (1865–1936); PRINCESS MARY (1897–1965); PRINCE EDWARD (1894–1972); QUEEN MARY (1867–1953)

SIR JOHN LAVERY, 1913
Oil on canvas, 3403 x 2718mm
NPG 1745

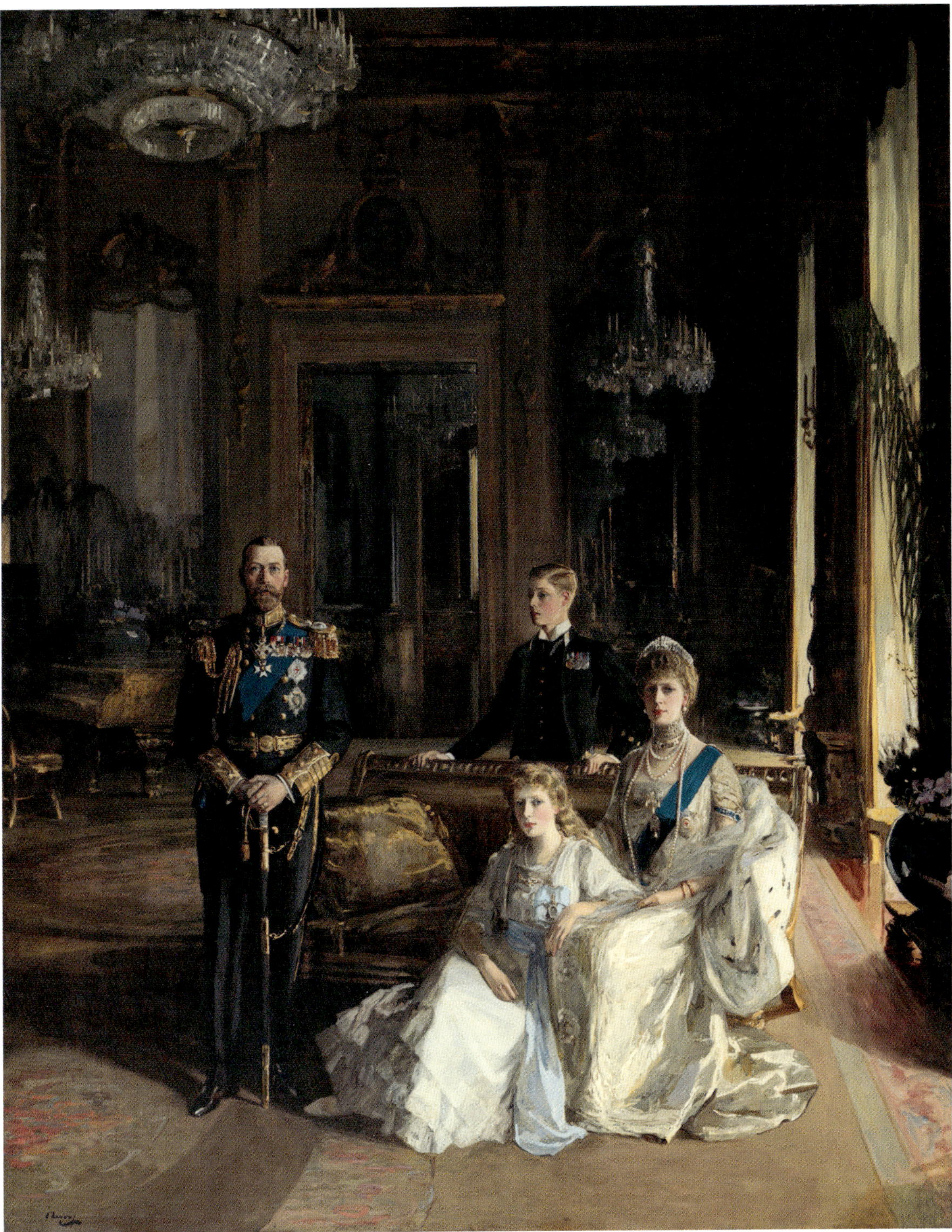

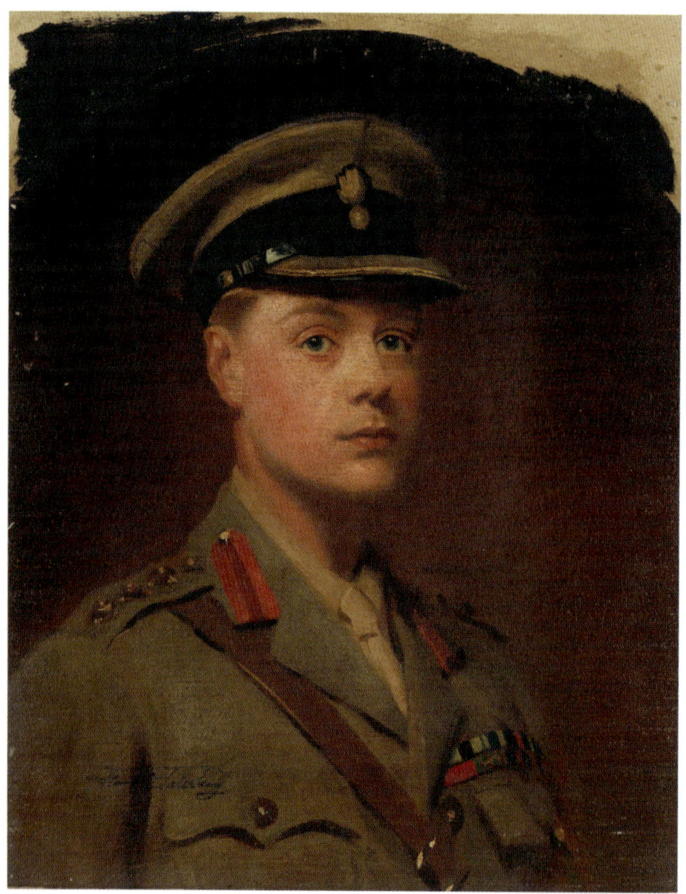

Edward (r.1936) was the eldest son of George V and Queen Mary. He had wanted to serve on the front line during the First World War but was refused due to the danger that it posed. He instead spent most of the war visiting the troops. This portrait was painted during a visit to the Western Front in France, in September 1917.

Charm and good looks increased Edward's popularity with the public, both at home and abroad. He succeeded his father as King Edward VIII in January 1936. Edward reigned for less than a year before abdicating – a constitutional crisis brought about by his determination to marry Wallis Simpson. As a twice-divorced American, the British establishment considered her unsuitable as queen.

Edward abdicated before his coronation and before an official portrait could be painted. After the couple married in 1937, they were styled the Duke and Duchess of Windsor and lived primarily in France, with relatively little contact with the new royal family.

[65]
KING EDWARD VIII
FRANK SALISBURY, 1917

Oil on board, 635 x 505mm
NPG 7006

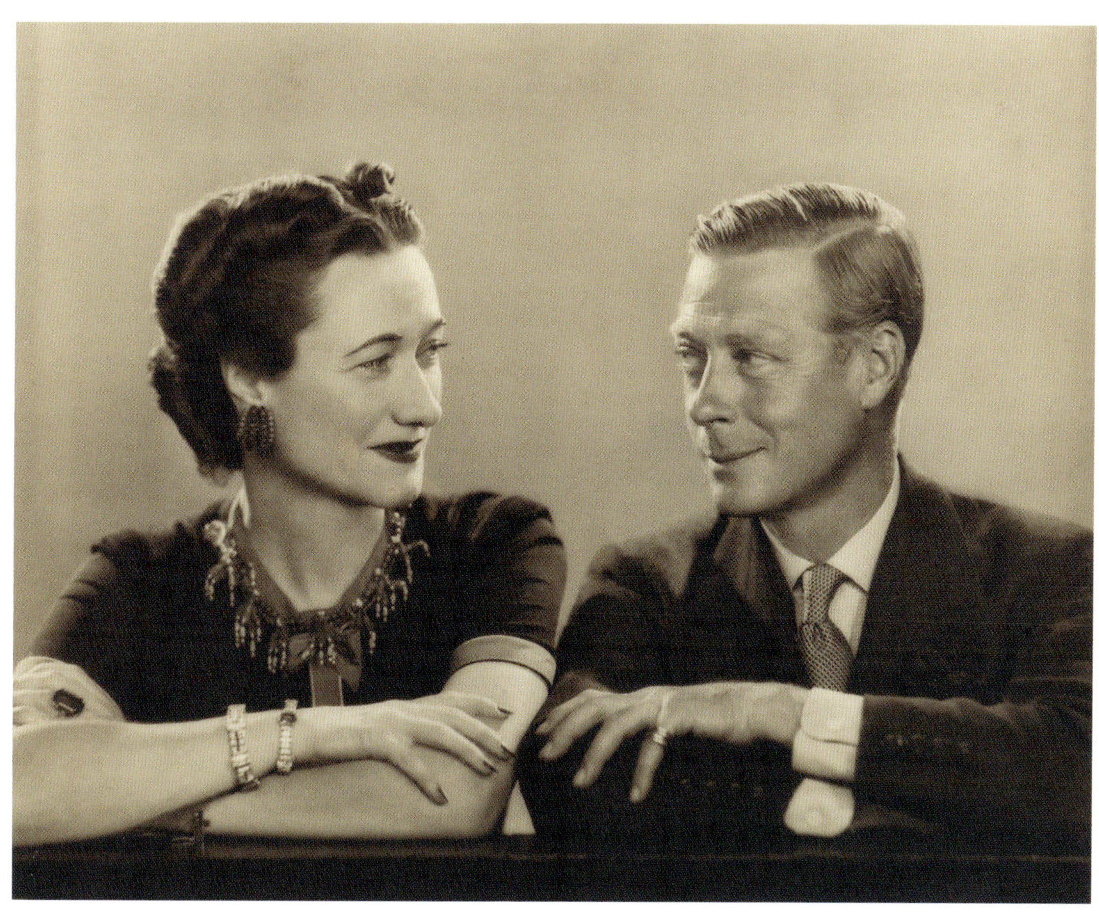

[66]
WALLIS, DUCHESS OF WINDSOR AND KING EDWARD VIII
(1896–1986; 1894–1972)
DOROTHY WILDING, 1943

Gelatin silver print, 225 x 283mm
NPG x35856

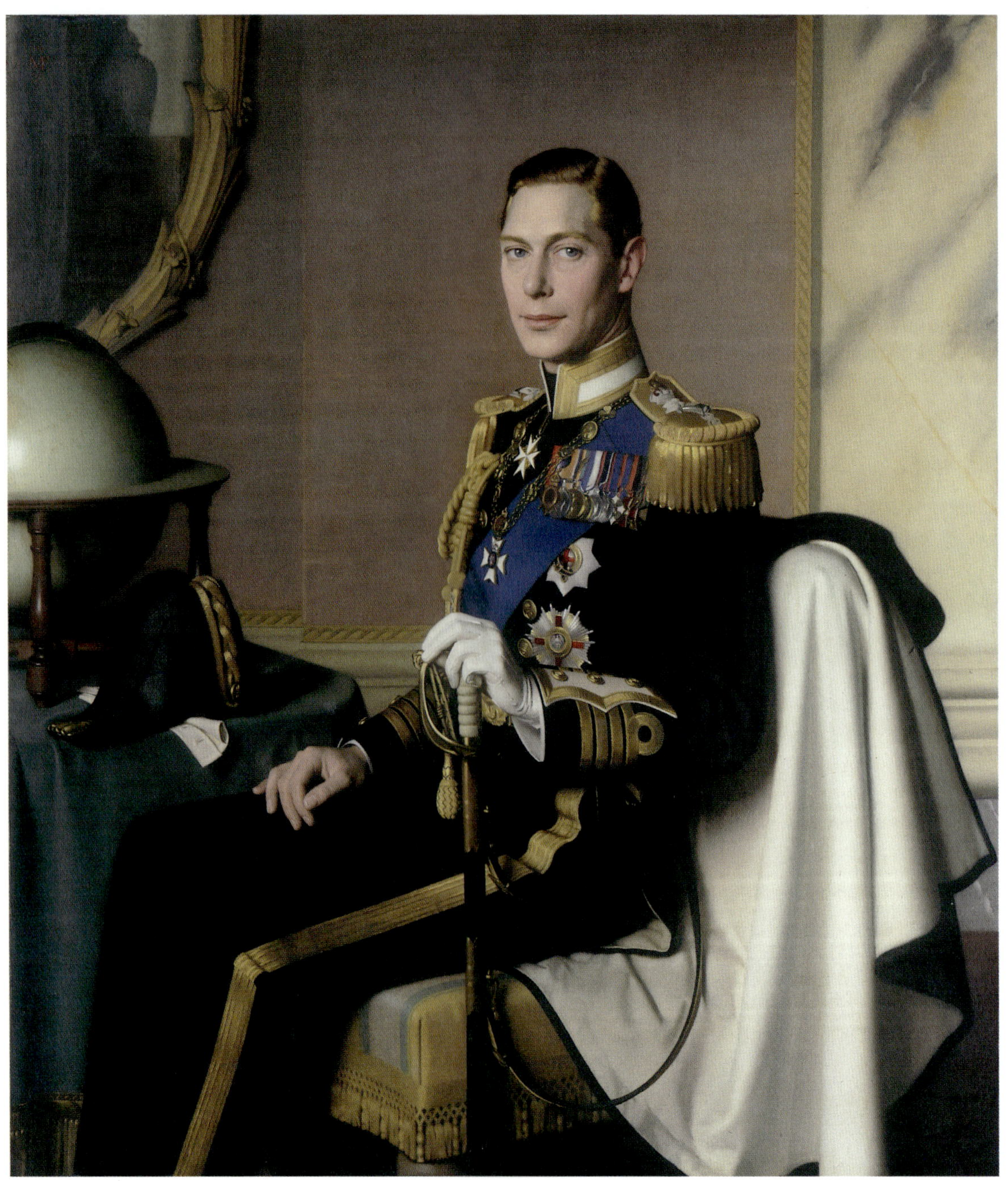

George (r.1936–52) was the second son of George V and Queen Mary. He served with distinction in the navy and air force during the First World War. His service medals are proudly displayed in this portrait of him in his Royal Navy uniform. George had grown up in his older brother Edward's shadow and suffered from a serious stammer that made official duties as Duke of York difficult. He married Elizabeth Bowes-Lyon in 1923 and they had two daughters, Elizabeth and Margaret.

Upon Edward VIII's abdication in 1936, George unexpectedly became king. Within three years of acceding to the throne, he was faced with the challenge of leading the nation during the Second World War. By refusing to leave London throughout the bombing, and visiting the sites affected by the Blitz, he did much to boost public morale.

After the war, George presided over major changes at home and abroad, including the beginning of the dismantling of the British Empire, marked by the independence of India in 1947. George enjoyed great popularity and his reign brought stability to the monarchy after the abdication crisis.

[67]
KING GEORGE VI
(1895–1952)
MEREDITH FRAMPTON, 1929

Oil on canvas, 1334 x 1188mm
NPG L214

Elizabeth Bowes-Lyon, daughter of the Earl and Countess of Strathmore and Kinghorne, became queen in 1936, when her husband acceded the throne as George VI upon the abdication of his brother Edward VIII. Along with their two children, Elizabeth and Margaret, the queen supported George with his new duties as king.

Upon George's death, she assumed the style of Queen Elizabeth, the Queen Mother. Retaining impressive vigour and popularity, she carried out public engagements long into her old age, and was the first member of a European royal family to become a centenarian.

This group portrait celebrating the royal family unit was commissioned by the National Portrait Gallery. The king and queen were widely praised for choosing to stay in London during the Second World War despite Buckingham Palace being bombed during the Blitz.

[68]
'CONVERSATION PIECE AT THE ROYAL LODGE, WINDSOR'
KING GEORGE VI (1895–1952); QUEEN ELIZABETH, THE QUEEN MOTHER (1900–2002); QUEEN ELIZABETH II (1926–2022); PRINCESS MARGARET (1930–2002)

SIR JAMES GUNN, 1950
Oil on canvas, 1511 x 1003mm
NPG 3778

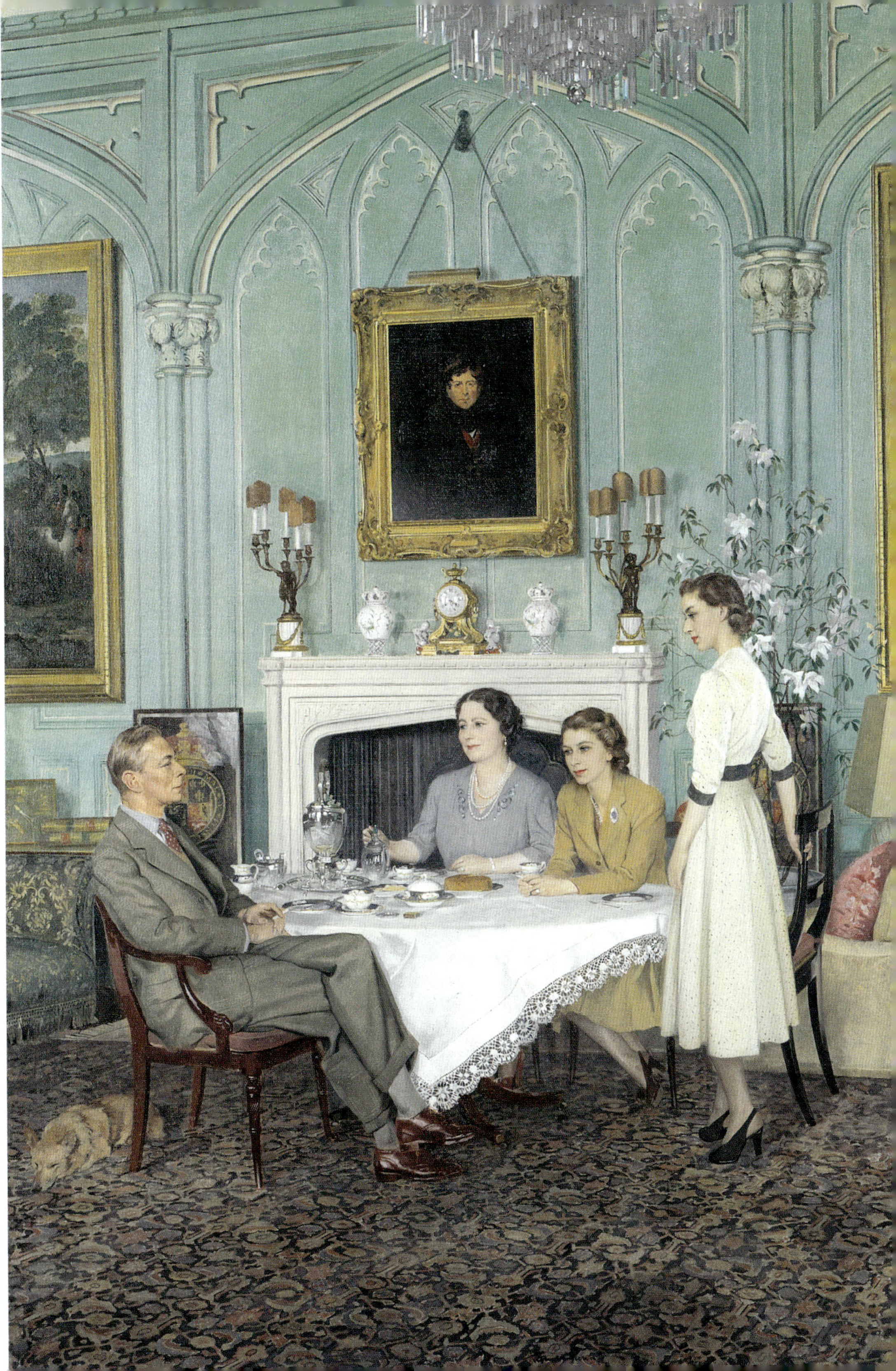

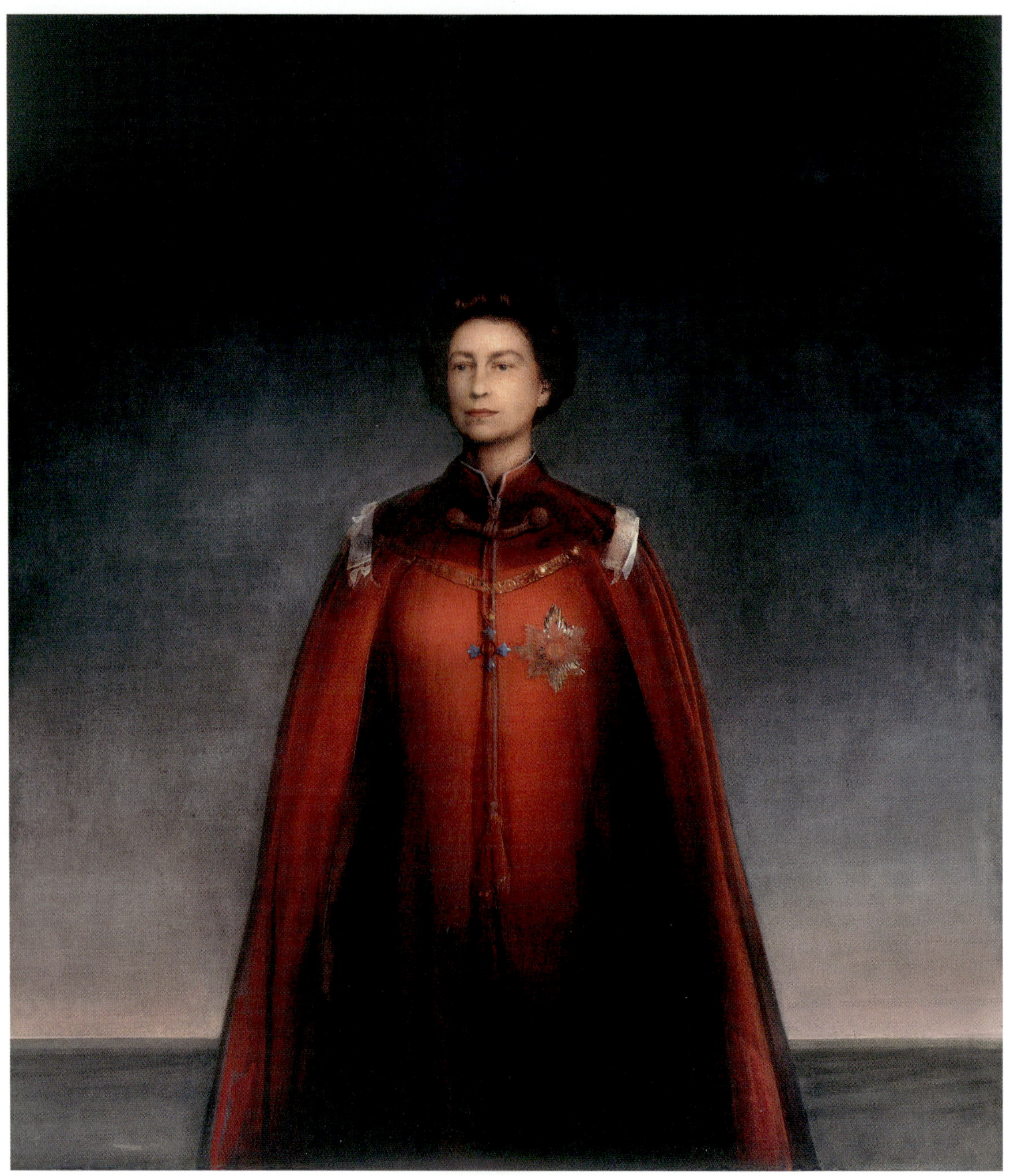

Queen Elizabeth II (r.1952–2022) succeeded to the throne at the age of 25, and her ascension was welcomed as a new Elizabethan era following years of post-war austerity. Her reign spanned 70 years of huge social and cultural change, including the dismantling of the British Empire and the establishment of the Commonwealth of Nations.

Respected internationally, and enormously popular in Britain, she became Britain's longest reigning monarch in 2015, having been queen at that point for 63 years. In 2022, Elizabeth celebrated her Platinum Jubilee. Her death at the age of 96 in October of that year provoked widespread mourning.

In this monumental portrait, she wears the robes of the Order of the British Empire. It was commissioned by the National Portrait Gallery, and the queen expressed a preference for Pietro Annigoni, who had painted her once before. The artist noted 'I did not want to paint her as a film star; I saw her as a monarch, alone in the problems of her responsibility.'

[69]
QUEEN ELIZABETH II
(1926–2022)
PIETRO ANNIGONI, 1969

Tempera grassa on paper on panel, 1981 x 1778mm
NPG 4706

Philip was the only son of Andrew of Greece and Denmark and Alice of Battenberg. He was the nephew of the former king of Greece, Constantine I, and a descendant of Queen Victoria. During the Second World War, Philip served in the Royal Navy, and he and Princess Elizabeth became engaged shortly afterwards. On their marriage, the prince renounced his own foreign royal titles and was made Duke of Edinburgh. The couple had four children.

This joint portrait was commissioned by the National Portrait Gallery to mark the Queen's Diamond Jubilee. The couple are posed in the Green Drawing Room at Windsor Castle shortly before Prince Philip's 90th birthday and during what was the 64th year of their marriage.

Philip was the patron of over 750 organisations, including The Duke of Edinburgh Award and the World Wide Fund for Nature.

[70]
PRINCE PHILIP, DUKE OF EDINBURGH AND QUEEN ELIZABETH II
(1921–2021; 1926–2022)
THOMAS STRUTH, 7 APRIL 2011

Chromogenic print, 1633 x 2062mm
NPG P1665

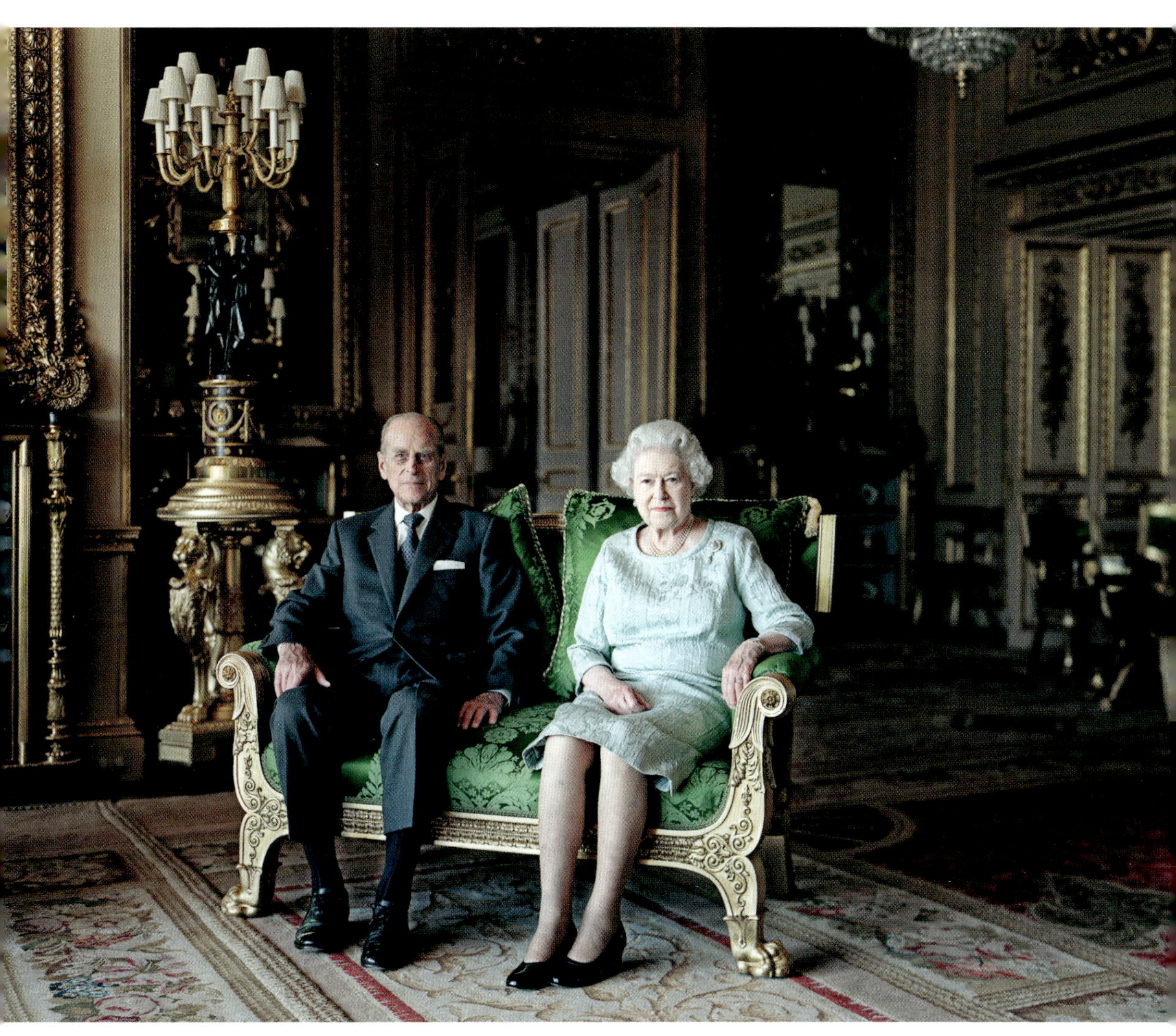

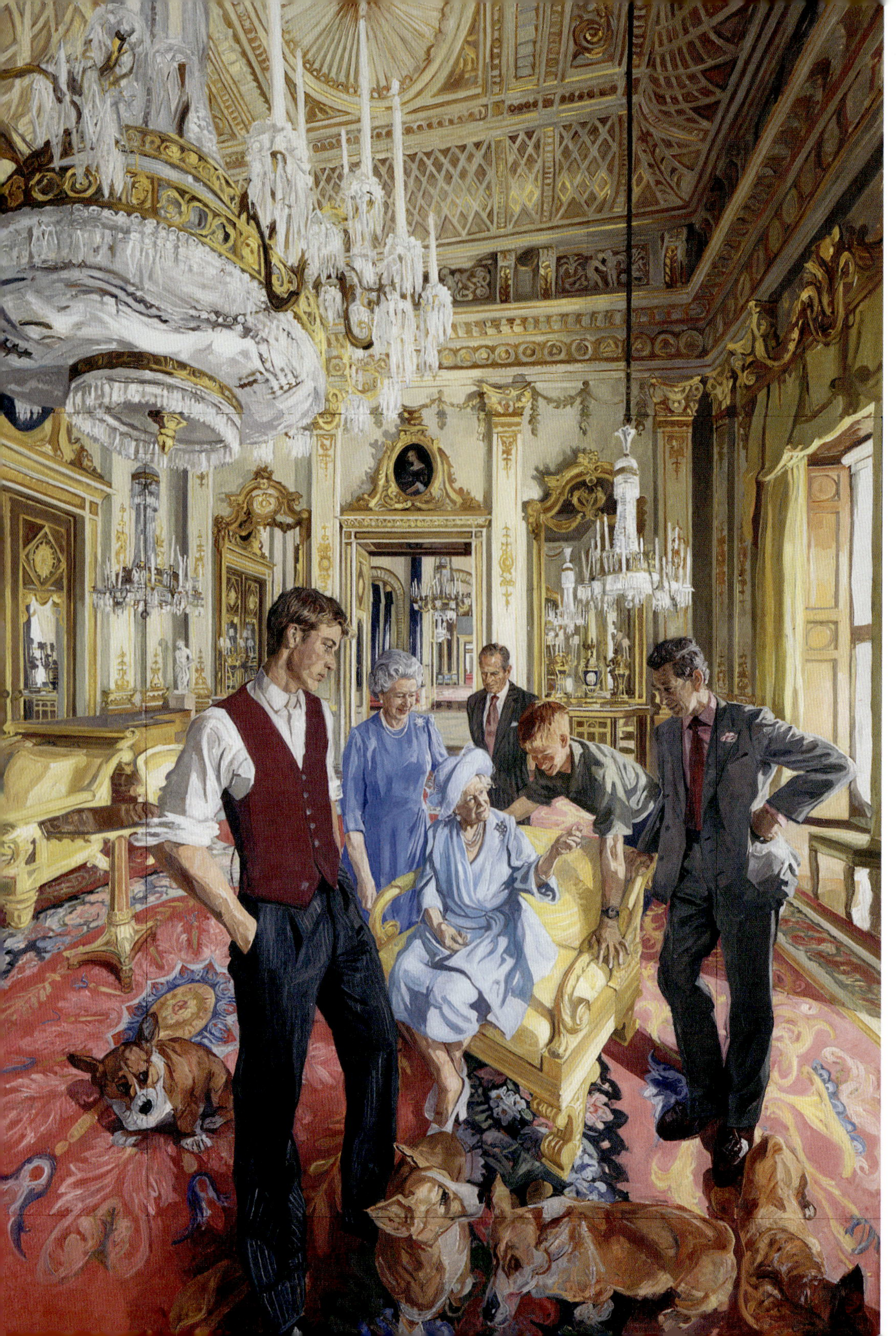

Commissioned by the National Portrait Gallery to celebrate the 100th birthday of the Queen Mother, this portrait of four generations of royals was suggested by the artist himself, as a way of immortalising the royal family on the eve of a new millennium. John Wonnacott depicts his sitters in the White Drawing Room at Buckingham Palace, consciously emulating in setting and scale Lavery's portrait of George V and the royal family from 1913 (p.111).

[71]
'THE ROYAL FAMILY: A CENTENARY PORTRAIT'
WILLIAM, THE PRINCE OF WALES (b.1982); QUEEN ELIZABETH II (1926–2022); QUEEN ELIZABETH, THE QUEEN MOTHER (1900–2002); PRINCE PHILIP, DUKE OF EDINBURGH (1921–2021); PRINCE HARRY, DUKE OF SUSSEX (b.1984); KING CHARLES III (b.1948)

JOHN WONNACOTT, 2000
Oil on canvas, 3663 x 2493mm
NPG 6479

Charles (r.2022–) is the oldest son of Elizabeth II and Prince Philip. He served in the Royal Air Force and Royal Navy from 1971 to 1976. Soon after, he founded the Prince's Trust, a youth charity that offers support, mentoring and advice. Since then, Charles has established over a dozen more Prince's Trust organisations, while also being a patron of over 400 other charities.

Charles married Lady Diana Spencer in 1981. They had two sons, William and Harry. The relationship, which came under intense media scrutiny, deteriorated and the couple separated in 1992, divorcing four years later. He married Camilla Parker Bowles in 2005.

Charles was Britain's longest serving heir apparent before he acceded the throne upon the death of his mother, Elizabeth II, on 8 September 2022. The coronation of King Charles III and Queen Camilla took place at Westminster Abbey on 6 May 2023.

[72]
KING CHARLES III
(b.1948)
NADAV KANDER, 2013

Chromogenic print, 1565 x 1220mm
NPG P1989

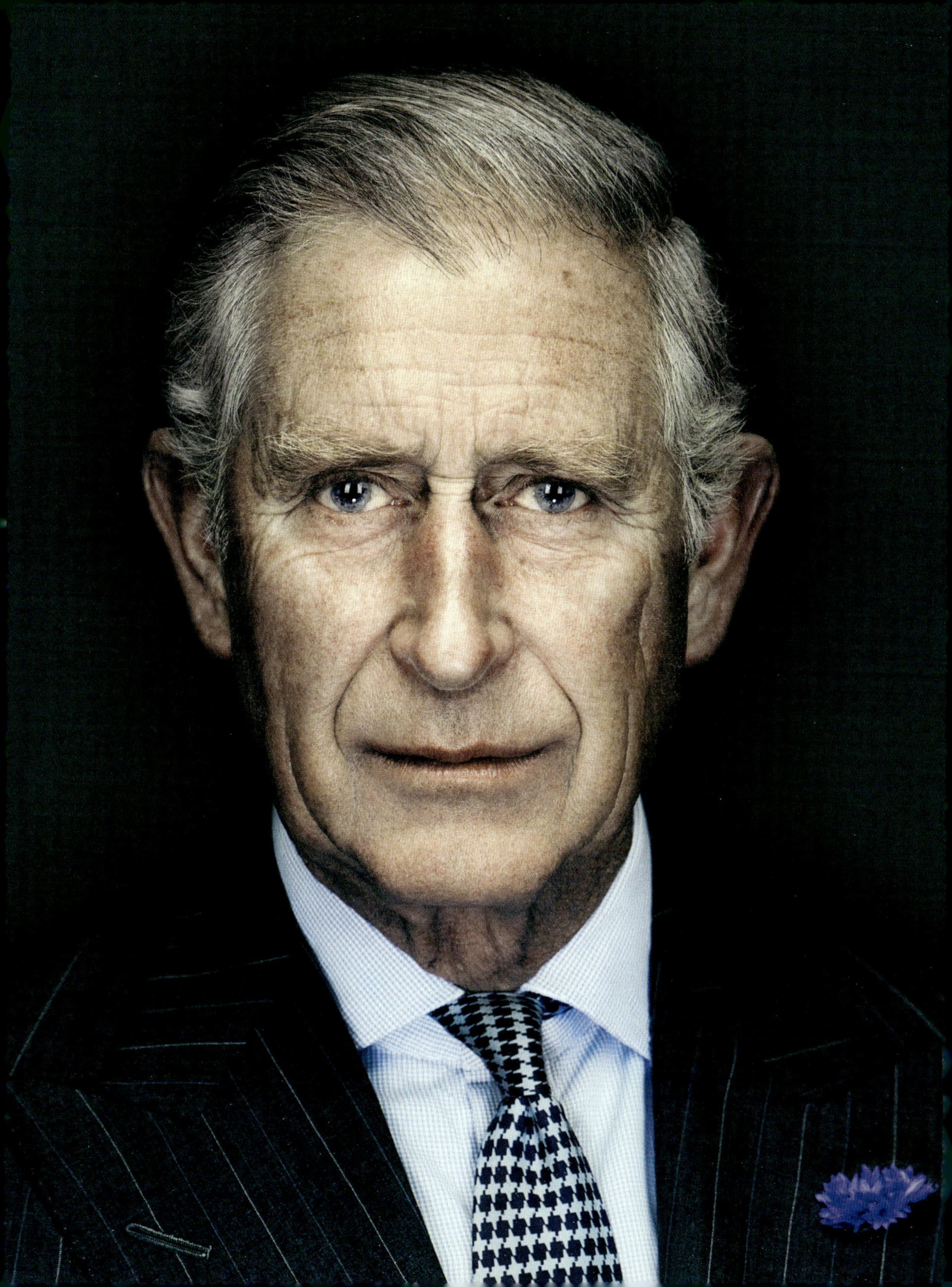

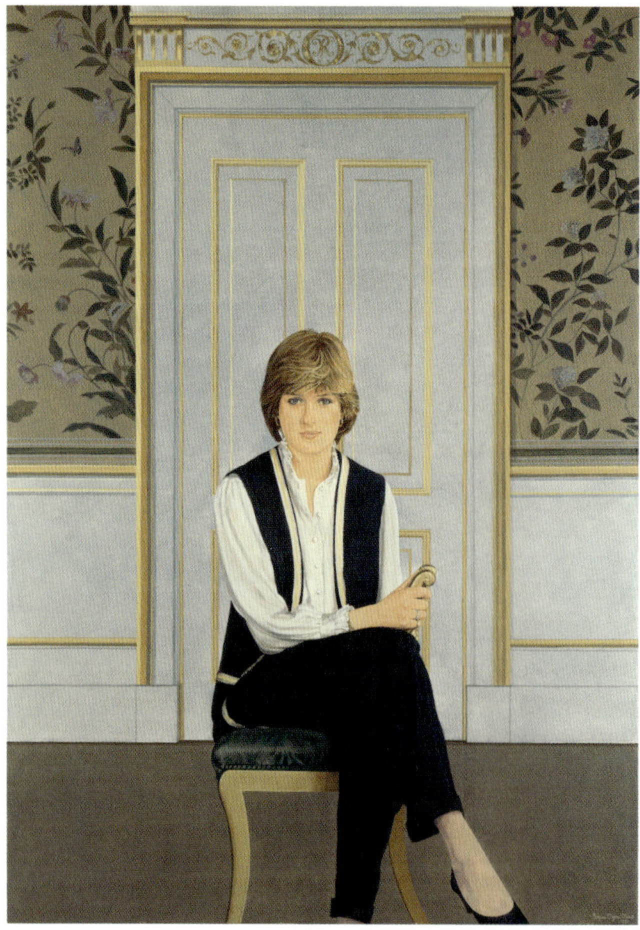

Diana was the youngest daughter of Frances and John Spencer (later 8th Earl Spencer). She married King Charles III – then Prince of Wales – in 1981, in a ceremony that was broadcast internationally to 750 million viewers. The couple had two sons, William and Harry, before divorcing in 1996.

Diana, Princess of Wales, enjoyed tremendous popularity. She was renowned for her charity work and for raising awareness around AIDS and the use of landmines.

One of the most photographed people of her time, Princess Diana generated global interest and was constantly followed by paparazzi. Her death in a car crash in 1997 at the age of 36 shocked the world and sparked a remarkable outpouring of public grief.

Commissioned to mark her engagement, Diana is shown here in the Yellow Drawing Room at Buckingham Palace. At the time, it was thought radical for a princess to be portrayed in a royal portrait wearing trousers.

The sense of informality that Diana brought to the royal family is perfectly captured in this photograph of her with her sons (p.127).

[73]
DIANA, PRINCESS OF WALES
BRYAN ORGAN, 1981

Acrylic on canvas, 1778 x 1270mm
NPG 5408

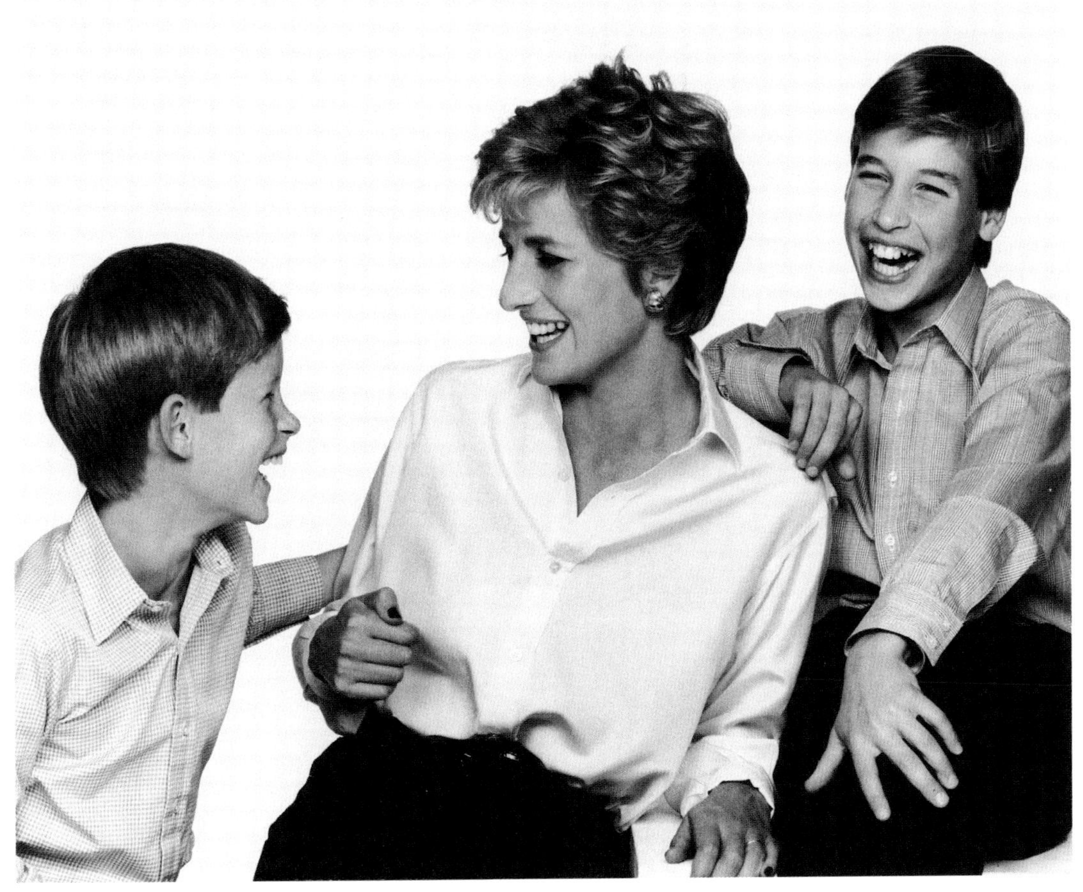

[74]
DIANA, PRINCESS OF WALES WITH HER SONS
PRINCE HARRY, DUKE OF SUSSEX (b.1984);
DIANA, PRINCESS OF WALES (1961–97);
WILLIAM, THE PRINCE OF WALES (b.1982)

JOHN SWANNELL, 1994
Inkjet print, 394 x 482mm
NPG P717(16)

Queen Camilla is the wife of King Charles III. Born Camilla Rosemary Shand, she was raised in East Sussex and South Kensington, London. She married Andrew Parker Bowles in 1973 and had two children, Tom and Laura, before divorcing in 1995.

Upon marrying Charles, then Prince of Wales, in 2005, Camilla became Duchess of Cornwall. She is president or patron of numerous charities and organisations and has campaigned to raise awareness about child literacy, animal welfare, sexual abuse and osteoporosis.

Photographed on the first anniversary of her wedding, Camilla appears relaxed and confident in the elegant surroundings of Clarence House, the London residence of the couple at the time. The pose, the choice of non-ceremonial clothes and her unguarded smile are all part of a more informal approach to royal portraiture embraced by the modern royal family.

[75]
QUEEN CAMILLA
(b.1947)
MARIO TESTINO, 2006

Chromogenic print, 1250 x 1670mm
NPG P1986

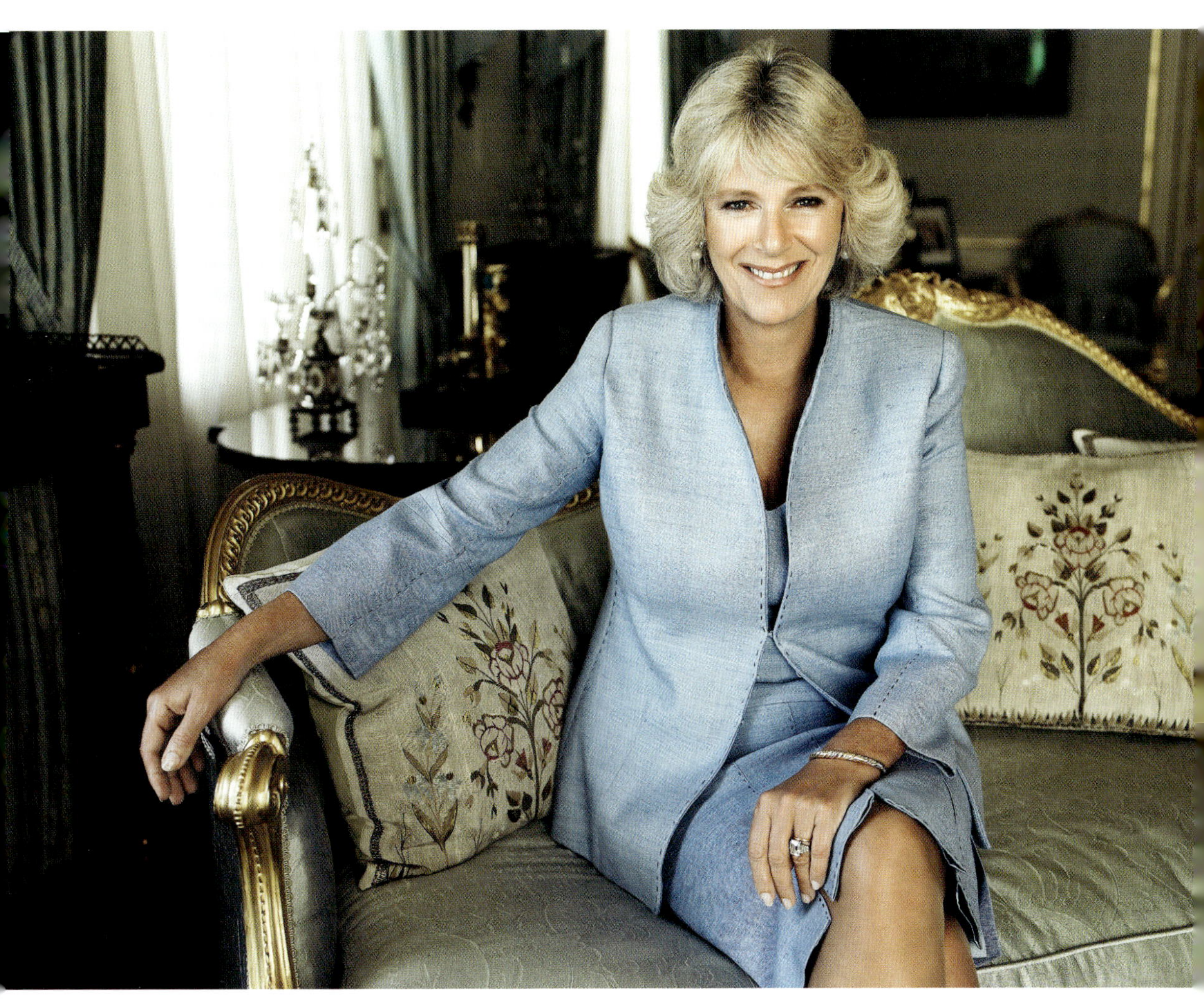

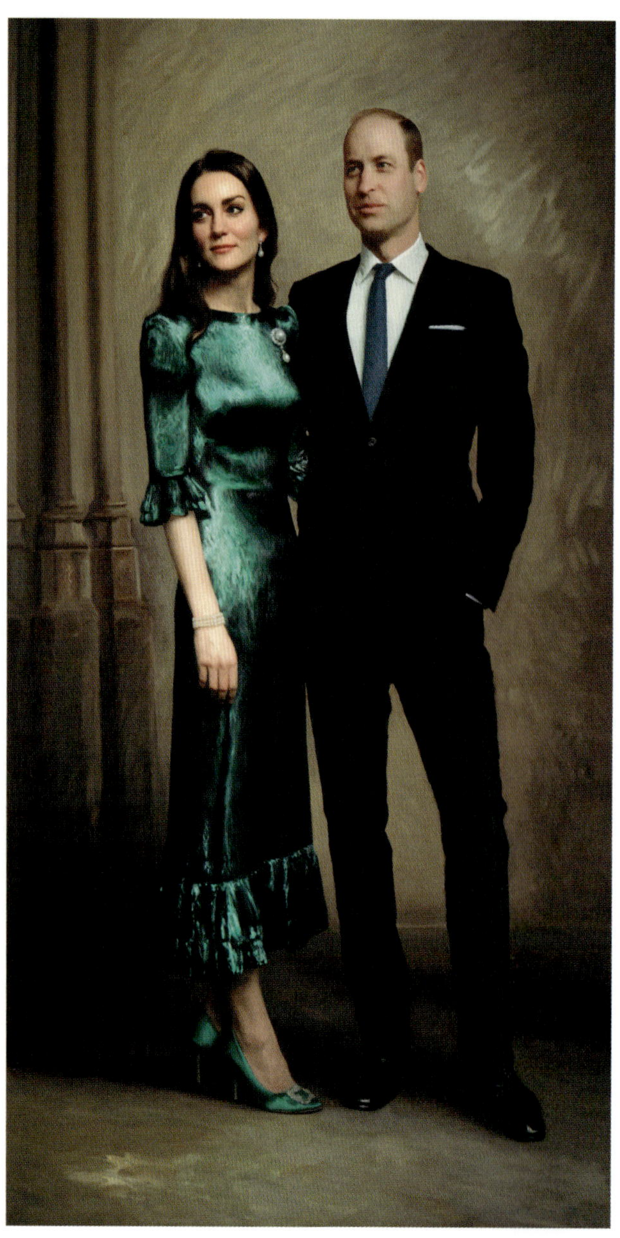

William, The Prince of Wales, is the eldest son of King Charles III and Diana, Princess of Wales, and is heir to the throne. He studied at St Andrews University in Scotland, where he met his wife, Catherine Middleton. They were married in 2011 and have three children: George, Charlotte and Louis. The couple have been praised for maintaining a balance between their royal duties and family life.

Since joining the Royal Military Academy Sandhurst as an Officer Cadet, The Prince of Wales has been a part of various British Armed Service organisations. Most recently, he contributed to the Royal Air Force as a Search and Rescue Pilot, and then went on to be an air ambulance pilot with the East Anglia Air Ambulance. The Prince is patron of over 30 military and charitable organisations.

[76]
THE DUKE AND DUCHESS OF CAMBRIDGE
CATHERINE, THE PRINCESS OF WALES (b.1982);
WILLIAM, THE PRINCE OF WALES (b.1982)
JAMIE CORETH, 2022

Oil on canvas, 2410 x 1411mm
Cambridgeshire Community Foundation

Catherine, The Princess of Wales, is the wife of William, The Prince of Wales. Upon their marriage, she became The Duchess of Cambridge. Her title changed to The Princess of Wales when King Charles III acceded to the throne in 2022.

The Princess of Wales is patron of 30 military and charitable organisations, including the National Portrait Gallery. It was there that she had her first solo public engagement, at the exhibition opening of *Lucian Freud Portraits* (2012). Catherine also collaborated with the Gallery on their exhibition *Victorian Giants: The Birth of Art Photography* (2018) and community project *Hold Still* (2021). A popular member of the royal family, The Princess of Wales has helped to usher in a new era for the monarchy.

This portrait was taken by Paolo Roversi to mark The Princess' 40th birthday.

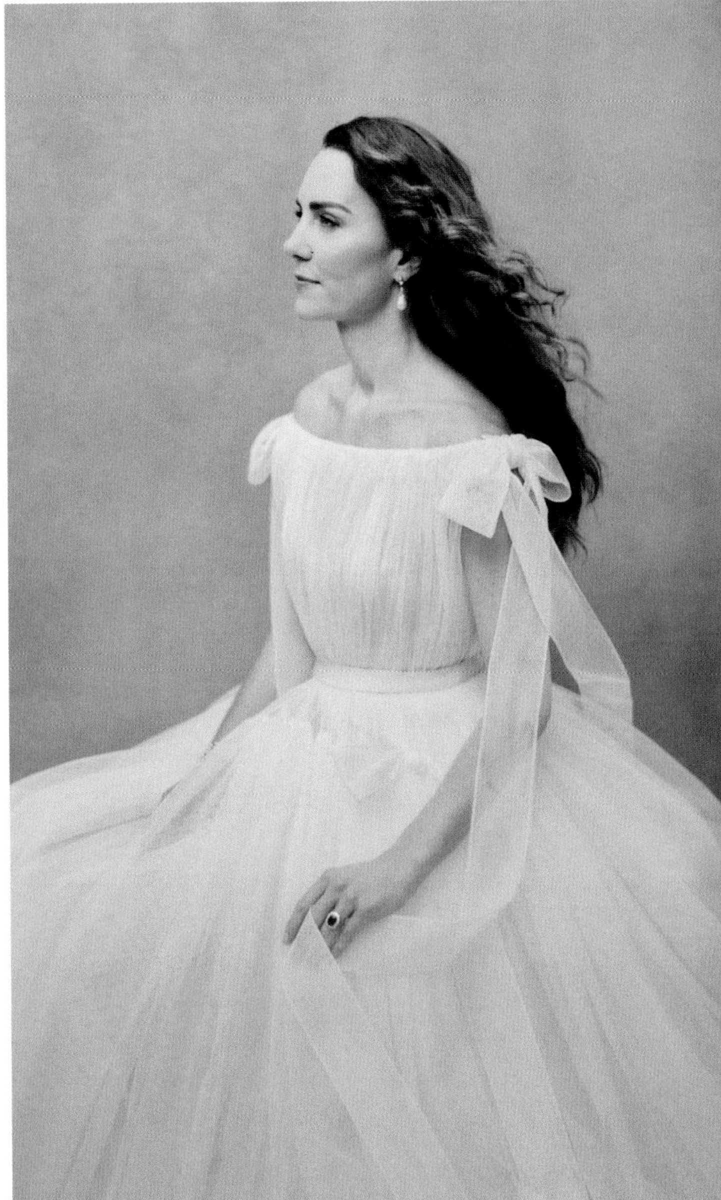

[77]
CATHERINE, THE PRINCESS OF WALES
PAOLO ROVERSI, 2021

Platinum palladium print, 500 x 330mm
NPG x201520

TIMELINE

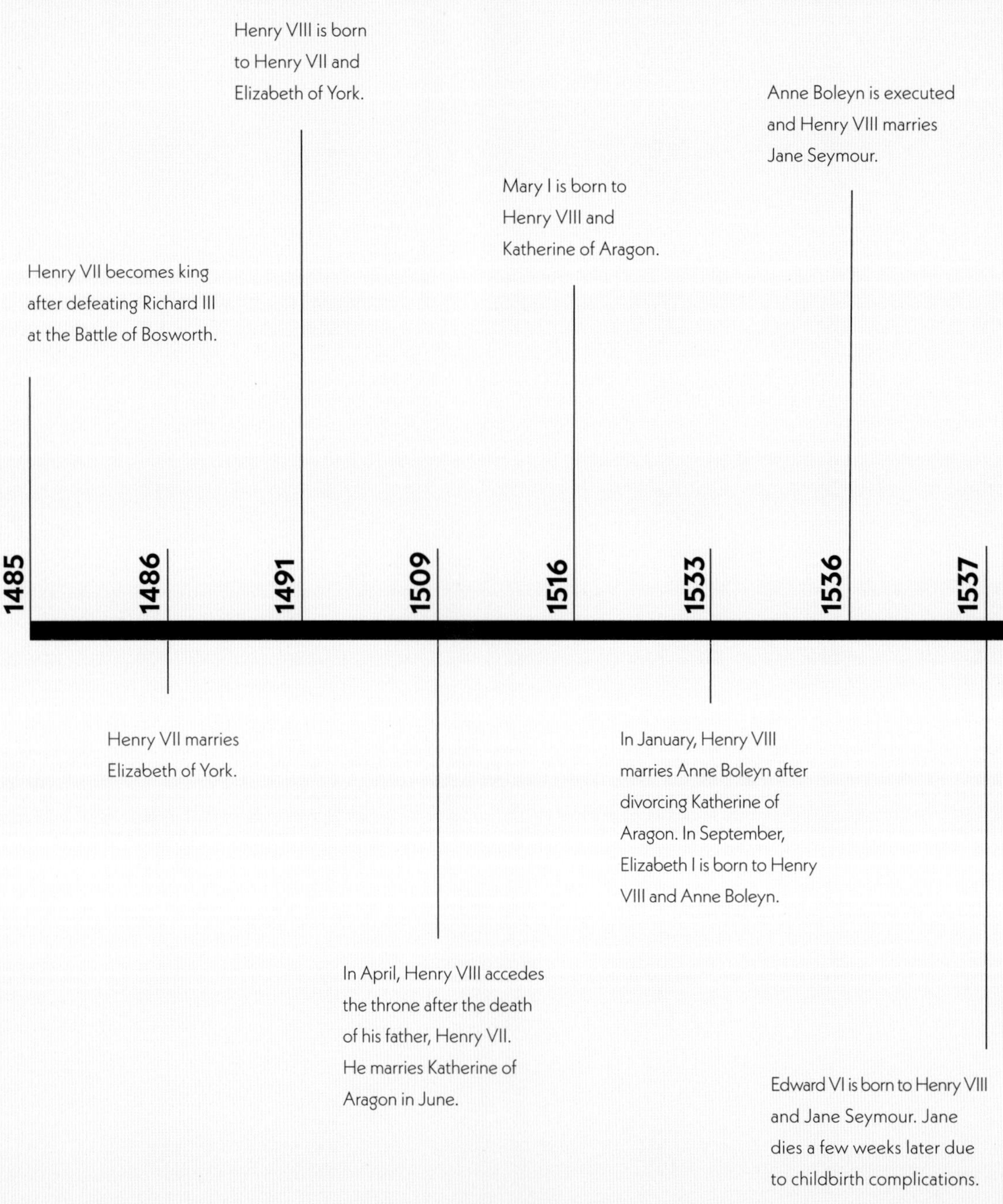
1485
Henry VII becomes king after defeating Richard III at the Battle of Bosworth.
1486
Henry VII marries Elizabeth of York.
1491
Henry VIII is born to Henry VII and Elizabeth of York.
1509
In April, Henry VIII accedes the throne after the death of his father, Henry VII. He marries Katherine of Aragon in June.
1516
Mary I is born to Henry VIII and Katherine of Aragon.
1533
In January, Henry VIII marries Anne Boleyn after divorcing Katherine of Aragon. In September, Elizabeth I is born to Henry VIII and Anne Boleyn.
1536
Anne Boleyn is executed and Henry VIII marries Jane Seymour.
1537
Edward VI is born to Henry VIII and Jane Seymour. Jane dies a few weeks later due to childbirth complications.

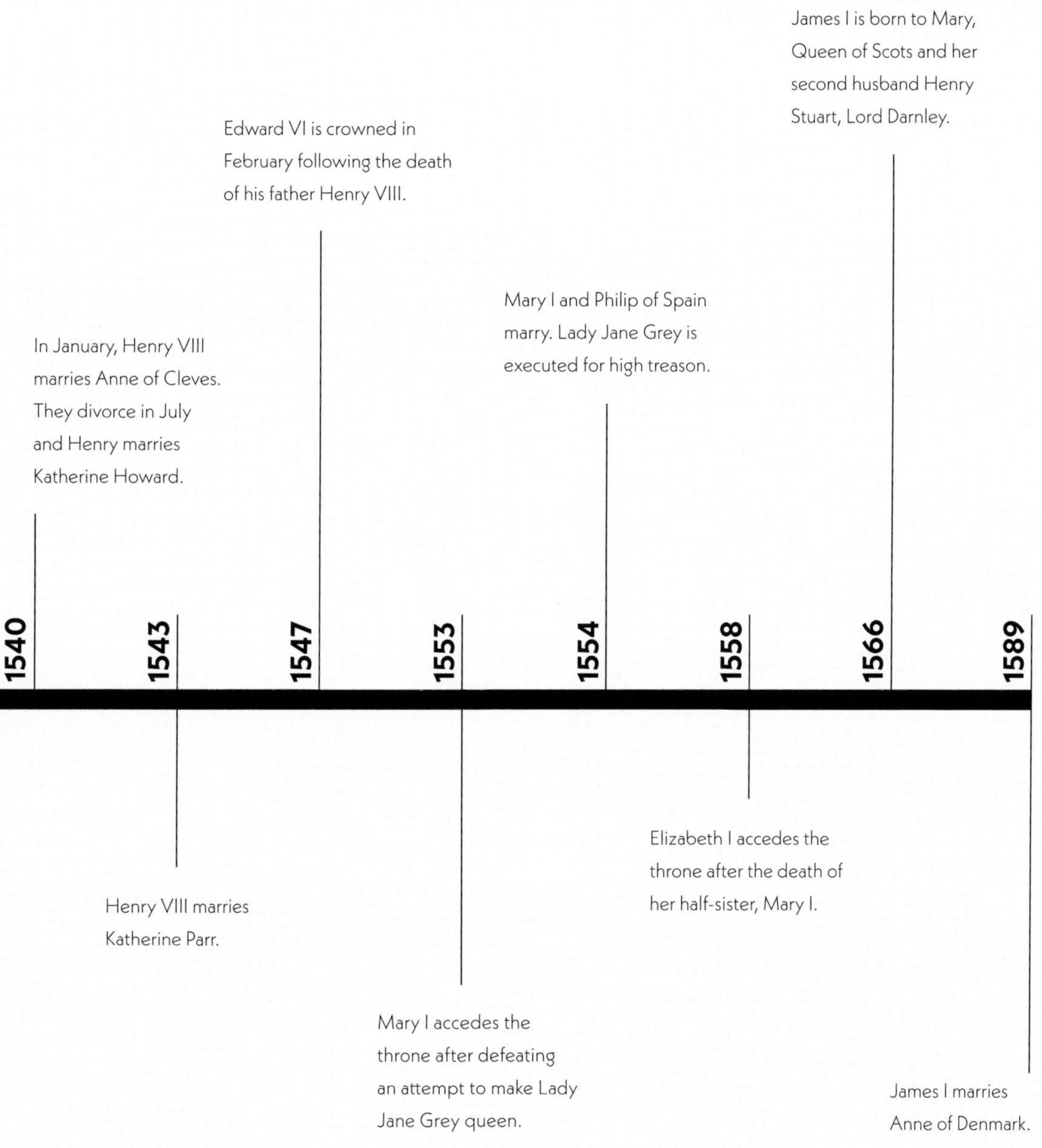
James I is born to Mary, Queen of Scots and her second husband Henry Stuart, Lord Darnley.
Edward VI is crowned in February following the death of his father Henry VIII.
Mary I and Philip of Spain marry. Lady Jane Grey is executed for high treason.
In January, Henry VIII marries Anne of Cleves. They divorce in July and Henry marries Katherine Howard.
1540
1543
1547
1553
1554
1558
1566
1589
Henry VIII marries Katherine Parr.
Elizabeth I accedes the throne after the death of her half-sister, Mary I.
Mary I accedes the throne after defeating an attempt to make Lady Jane Grey queen.
James I marries Anne of Denmark.

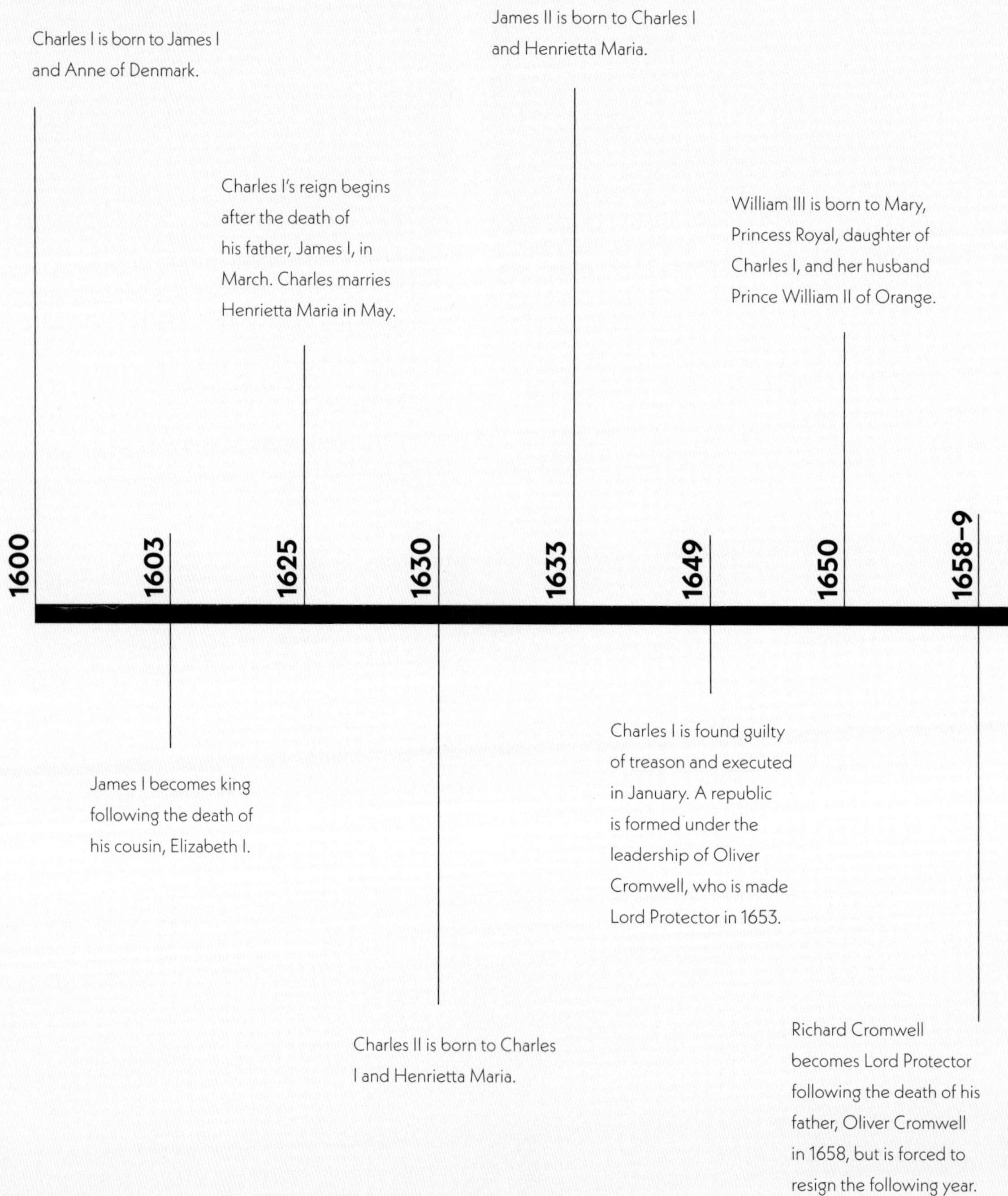
Charles I is born to James I and Anne of Denmark.
James II is born to Charles I and Henrietta Maria.
Charles I's reign begins after the death of his father, James I, in March. Charles marries Henrietta Maria in May.
William III is born to Mary, Princess Royal, daughter of Charles I, and her husband Prince William II of Orange.
1600
1603
1625
1630
1633
1649
1650
1658–9
James I becomes king following the death of his cousin, Elizabeth I.
Charles I is found guilty of treason and executed in January. A republic is formed under the leadership of Oliver Cromwell, who is made Lord Protector in 1653.
Charles II is born to Charles I and Henrietta Maria.
Richard Cromwell becomes Lord Protector following the death of his father, Oliver Cromwell in 1658, but is forced to resign the following year.

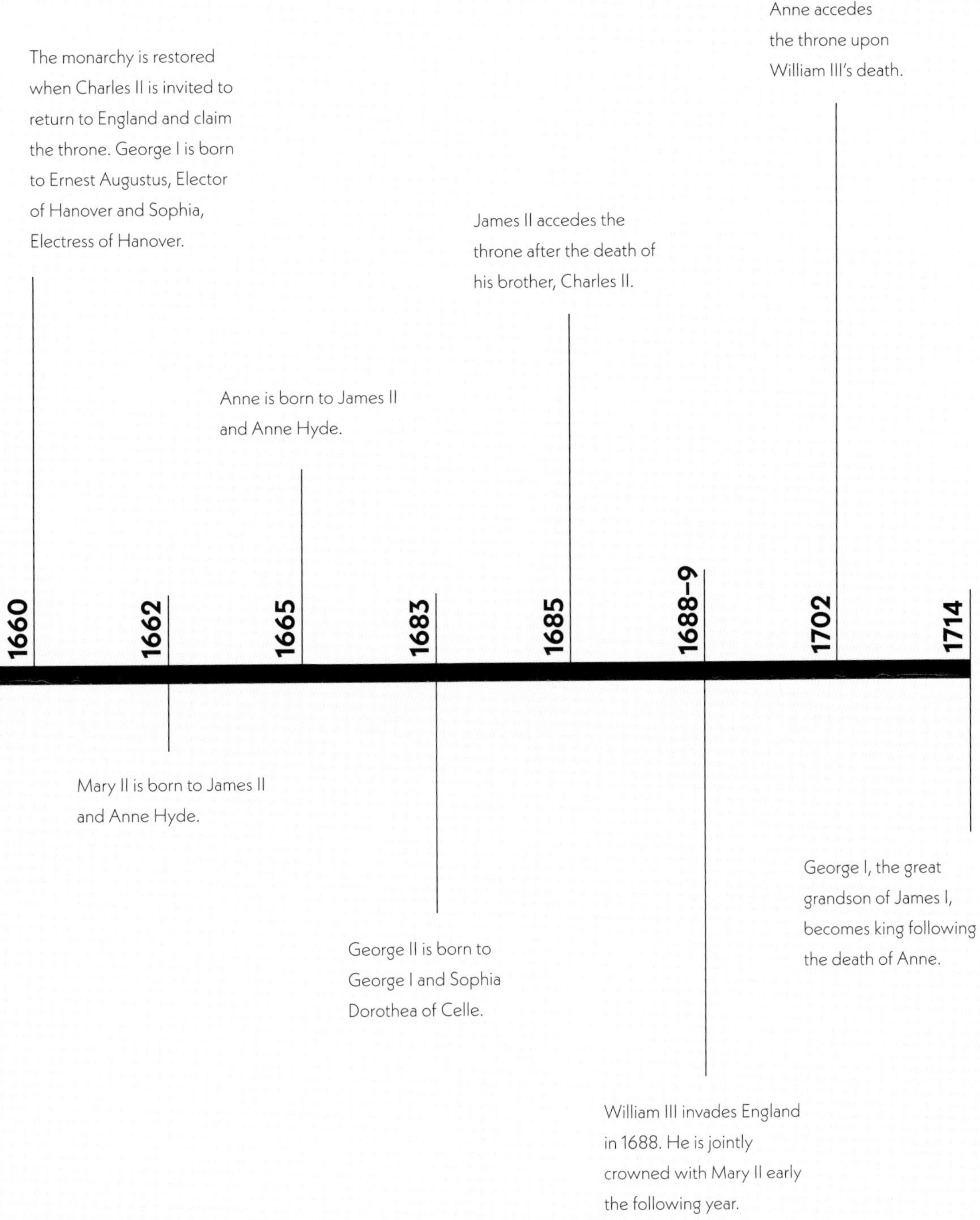
The monarchy is restored when Charles II is invited to return to England and claim the throne. George I is born to Ernest Augustus, Elector of Hanover and Sophia, Electress of Hanover.
1660
1662
Mary II is born to James II and Anne Hyde.
Anne is born to James II and Anne Hyde.
1665
1683
George II is born to George I and Sophia Dorothea of Celle.
James II accedes the throne after the death of his brother, Charles II.
1685
1688–9
William III invades England in 1688. He is jointly crowned with Mary II early the following year.
Anne accedes the throne upon William III's death.
1702
1714
George I, the great grandson of James I, becomes king following the death of Anne.

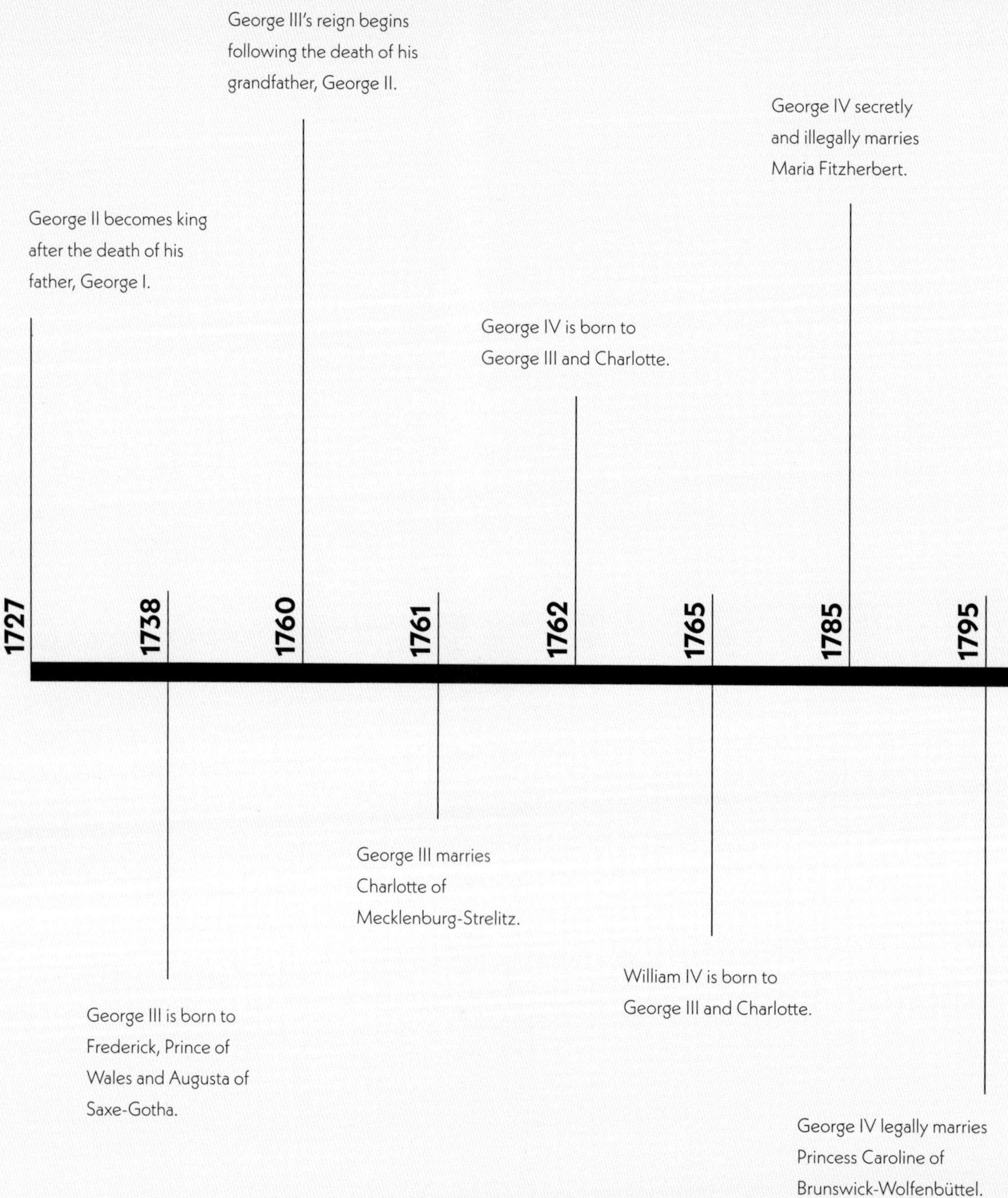
George II becomes king after the death of his father, George I.
1727
1738
George III is born to Frederick, Prince of Wales and Augusta of Saxe-Gotha.
George III's reign begins following the death of his grandfather, George II.
1760
1761
George III marries Charlotte of Mecklenburg-Strelitz.
George IV is born to George III and Charlotte.
1762
1765
William IV is born to George III and Charlotte.
George IV secretly and illegally marries Maria Fitzherbert.
1785
1795
George IV legally marries Princess Caroline of Brunswick-Wolfenbüttel.

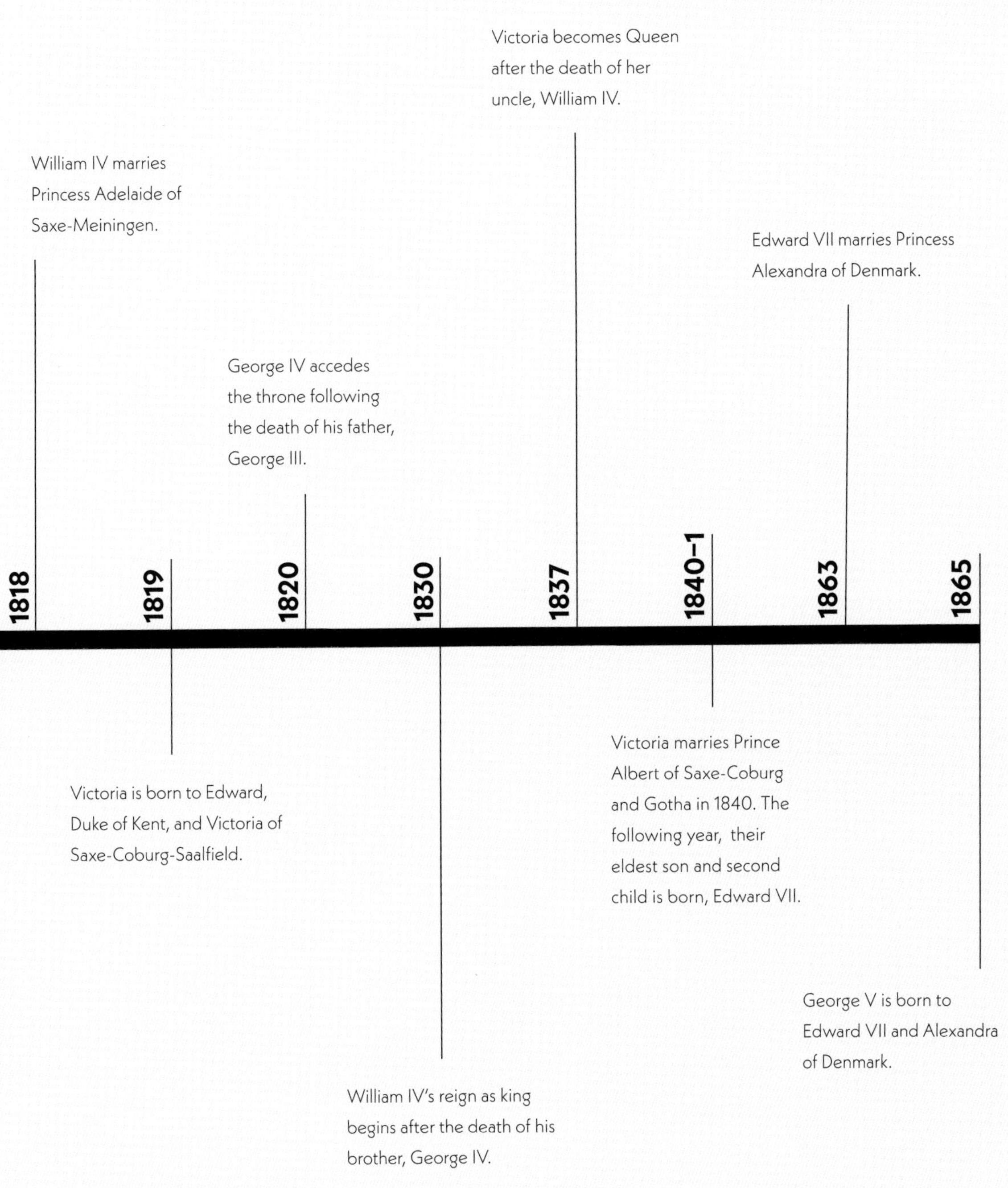
Victoria becomes Queen after the death of her uncle, William IV.
William IV marries Princess Adelaide of Saxe-Meiningen.
Edward VII marries Princess Alexandra of Denmark.
George IV accedes the throne following the death of his father, George III.
1818
1819
1820
1830
1837
1840–1
1863
1865
Victoria marries Prince Albert of Saxe-Coburg and Gotha in 1840. The following year, their eldest son and second child is born, Edward VII.
Victoria is born to Edward, Duke of Kent, and Victoria of Saxe-Coburg-Saalfield.
George V is born to Edward VII and Alexandra of Denmark.
William IV's reign as king begins after the death of his brother, George IV.

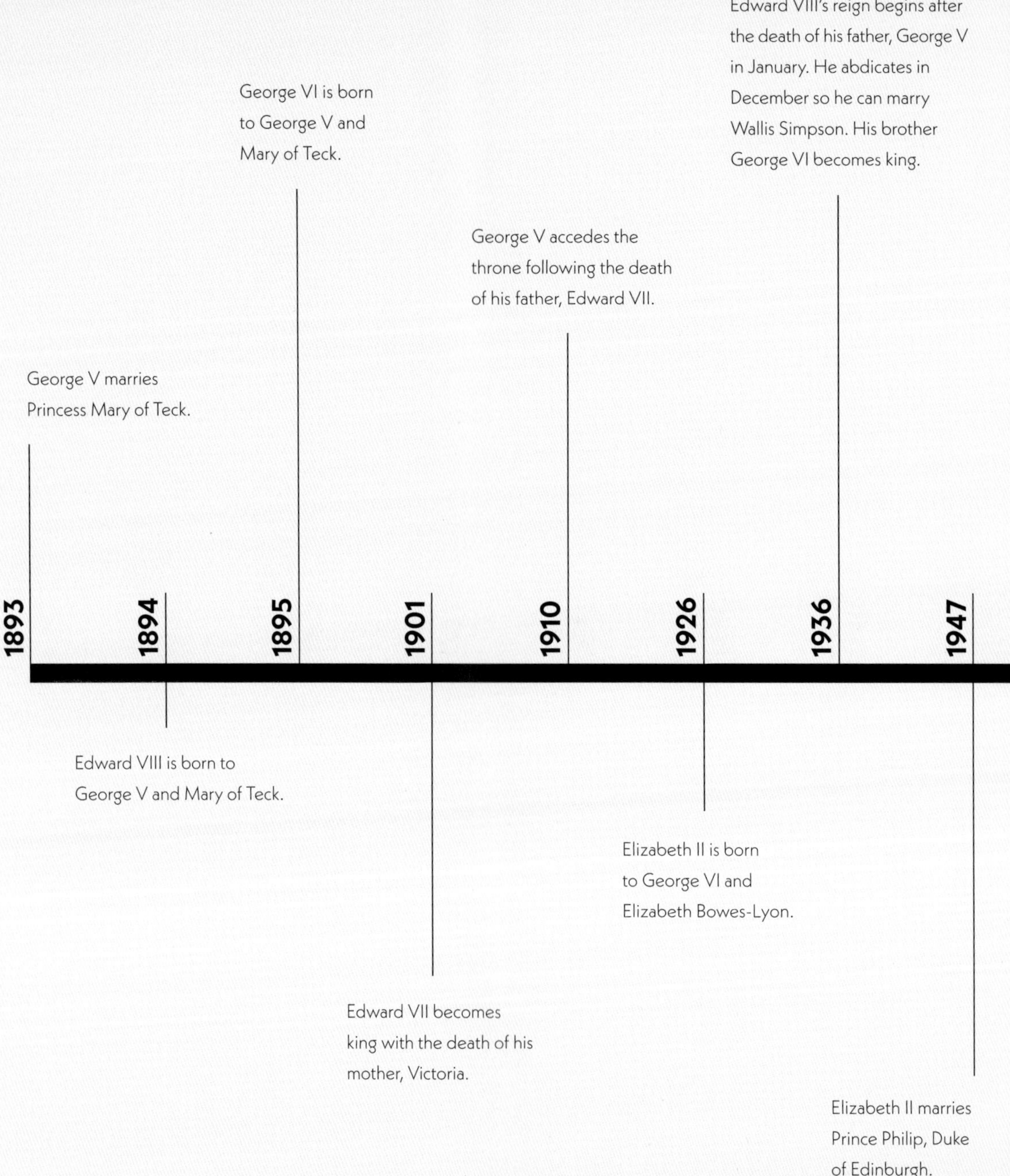
Edward VIII's reign begins after the death of his father, George V in January. He abdicates in December so he can marry Wallis Simpson. His brother George VI becomes king.
George VI is born to George V and Mary of Teck.
George V accedes the throne following the death of his father, Edward VII.
George V marries Princess Mary of Teck.
1893
1894
1895
1901
1910
1926
1936
1947
Edward VIII is born to George V and Mary of Teck.
Elizabeth II is born to George VI and Elizabeth Bowes-Lyon.
Edward VII becomes king with the death of his mother, Victoria.
Elizabeth II marries Prince Philip, Duke of Edinburgh.

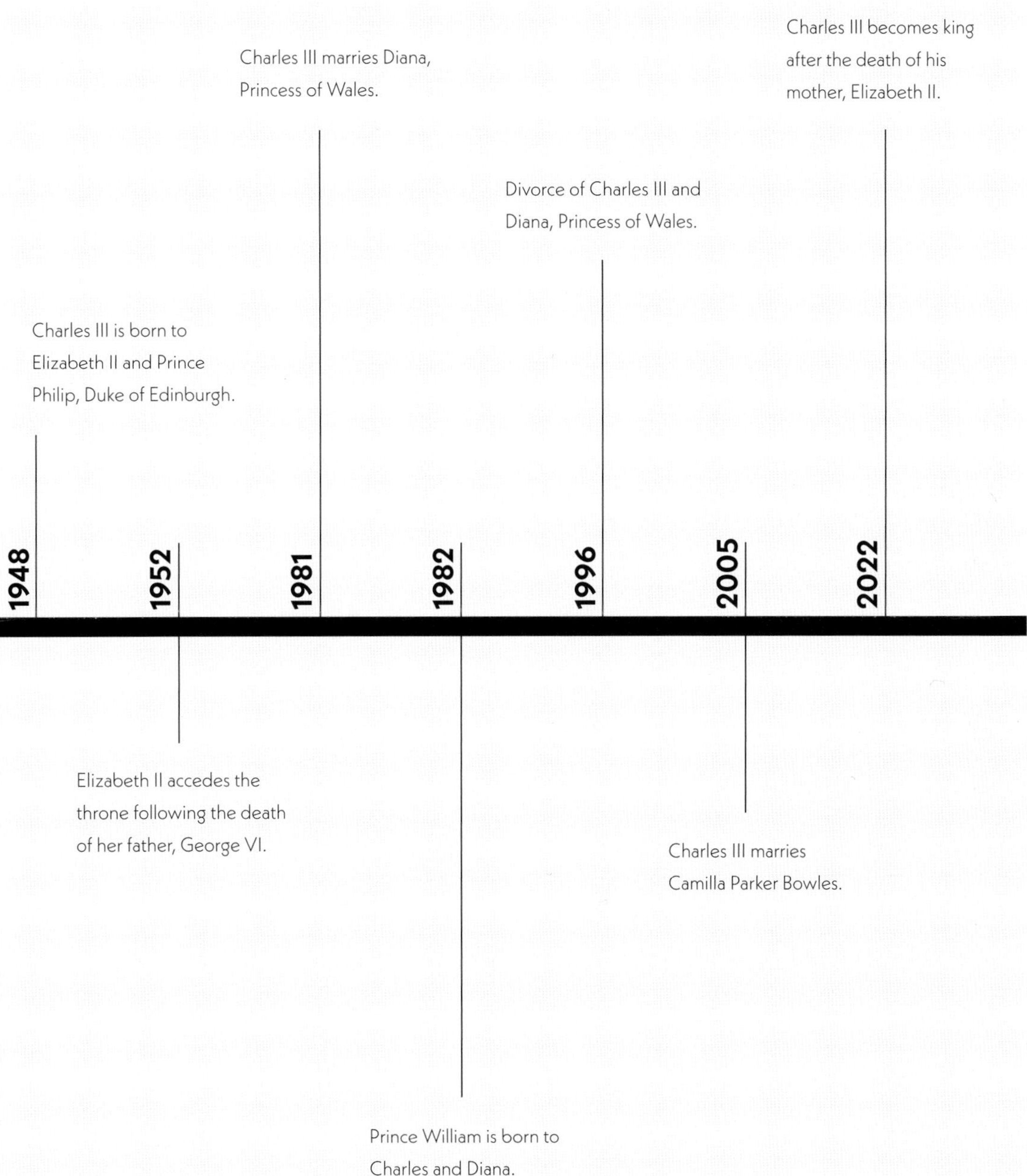
Charles III becomes king after the death of his mother, Elizabeth II.
Charles III marries Diana, Princess of Wales.
Divorce of Charles III and Diana, Princess of Wales.
Charles III is born to Elizabeth II and Prince Philip, Duke of Edinburgh.
1948
1952
1981
1982
1996
2005
2022
Elizabeth II accedes the throne following the death of her father, George VI.
Charles III marries Camilla Parker Bowles.
Prince William is born to Charles and Diana.

BIBLIOGRAPHY

The captions accompanying the images draw on material from a range of National Portrait Gallery publications and online resources, with further research contributed by curators Rab MacGibbon, Georgia Atienza, Tanya Bentley, Charlotte Bolland, Rosie Broadley, Paul Cox, Clare Freestone, Sarah Howgate, Sabina Jaskot-Gill, Catherine MacLeod, Sarah Moulden, Lucy Peltz, and Alison Smith.

Bolland, Charlotte, *The Tudors: Passion, Power, Politics* (2022)

Cannadine, David, *Tudors to Windsors: British Royal Portraits* (2018)

MacGibbon, Rab, *National Portrait Gallery: The Collection*, (2023)

Moorhouse, Paul, *The Queen: Art and Image* (2011)

Shulman, Alexandra, *Elizabeth II: Princess, Queen, Icon* (2022)

Smith, Alison, *Charles III: The Making of a King* (2023)

Williamson, David, *Kings and Queens* (2010)

npg.org.uk

PICTURE CREDITS

Unless otherwise stated, all illustrations are © National Portrait Gallery, London. Additional commissioning and acquisition information is provided. The National Portrait Gallery would like to thank the copyright holders for granting permission to reproduce works illustrated in this book. Every effort has been made to contact the holders of copyright material, and any omissions will be corrected in future editions if the publisher is notified in writing.

pp.2, 111 Given by William Hugh Spottiswoode, 1913
p.6 © Jason Bell. Purchased, 2014
p.10 © National Portrait Gallery, London. Given by James Thomson Gibson-Craig, 1862
pp.12, 42 Purchased with help from the Art Fund, 1965
p.15 © National Portrait Gallery, London (with contractual restrictions). Commissioned, 2009
p.22 © National Portrait Gallery, London, lent by permission of the Master and Fellows of St John's College, Cambridge. Lent by St John's College, Cambridge, 2023
p.26 By permission of the Archbishop of Canterbury and the Church Commissioners; on loan to the National Portrait Gallery, London
p.29 Given by Henry Witte Martin, 1861
p.30 Acquired, 1960 or earlier, from an unknown source
p.31 Purchased with help from the Gulbenkian Foundation, 1965
p.33 Purchased with help from the proceeds of the 150th anniversary gala, 2006
p.34 (left and right) Given by Edward Peter Jones, 1960
p.49 Given by Benjamin Seymour Guinness, 1952
p.50 Purchased with help from the Art Fund, 1966
p.54 Given by Henry Louis Bischoffsheim, 1899
p.56 Transferred from the British Museum, London, 1879
p.59 Bequeathed by Harold Lee-Dillon, 17th Viscount Dillon, 1933
p.60 Purchased with help from the National Heritage Memorial Fund, through the Art Fund (with a contribution from the Wolfson Foundation), Camelot Group plc, David and Catharine Alexander, David Wilson, E.A. Whitehead, Glyn Hopkin and numerous other supporters of a public appeal including members of the Chelsea Arts Club, 2005
p.61 Bequeathed by John Neale, 1931
p.81 Bequeathed by Miss Lillie Belle Randell, 1931
p.82 By consent of the owners; on loan to the National Portrait Gallery, London; photograph © National Portrait Gallery, London. Lent by a private collection, 1976
p.87 Purchased with help from the Art Fund, 1928
p.88 Transferred from Tate Gallery, 2015
p.95 Given by Queen Victoria, 1900
p.96 Given by Rhoda Helen ('Dodie') Masterman, 1964
p.97 Given by Queen Victoria, 1867
p.99 Given by King George V, 1912
p.100 Given by King George V, 1920
p.103 Purchased with help from the Friends of the National Libraries and the Pilgrim Trust, 1966
p.104 Given by the photographer's sister, Susan Morton, 1976
p.113 Given by the photographer's sister, Susan Morton, 1976
p.114 © National Portrait Gallery, London; private collection. Lent by Trustees of Barnardo's, 1997
p.117 Commissioned, 1950
p.118 Given by Sir Hugh Leggatt, 1970
p.121 © Thomas Struth, 2011. Commissioned, 2011
p.122 © John Wonnacott / National Portrait Gallery, London. Commissioned, 2000
p.125 © Nadav Kander. Purchased, 2015
p.126 Commissioned, 1981
p.127 © John Swannell / Camera Press. Given by the photographer, John Swannell, 1998
p.129 © Mario Testino. Purchased, 2015
p.130 © Cambridgeshire Community Foundation © Jamie Coreth and Fine Art Commissions Ltd. Courtesy of the Cambridgeshire Community Foundation, 2024
p.131 © Paolo Roversi / The Duchess of Cambridge released to mark the occasion of The Duchess's 40th birthday in January 2022. Given by Paolo Roversi, 2022

Published in Great Britain by
National Portrait Gallery Publications
National Portrait Gallery
St Martin's Place
London WC2H 0HE

Every purchase supports the National Portrait Gallery, London. For a complete catalogue of current publications, please visit our website at
www.npg.org.uk/publications

Front cover: *Queen Elizabeth I* by Nicholas Hilliard, *c*.1575

Back cover: *Conversation Piece at The Royal Lodge, Windsor* by Sir James Gunn, 1950

ISBN 978-1-85514-534-4

A catalogue record for this book is available from the British Library.

10 9 8 7 6 5 4 3 2 1

Director of Commercial: Anna Starling
Publishing Manager: Kara Green
Cross-Collections Curator: Rab MacGibbon
Project Editor: Jemma Jacobs
Production Controller: Priti Kothary
Design: Daniela Rocha
Proofreader: Sara Harrison
Printed in Italy by Printer Trento
Origination by DL Imaging

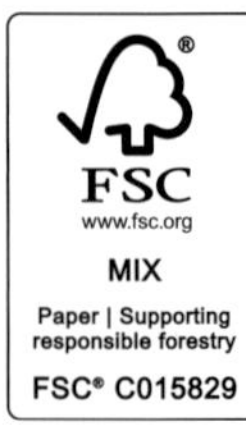